South of the Clouds

To Jane and Kim Stallings

SOUTH of the CLOUDS

TRAVELS IN SOUTHWEST CHINA

Bill Porter

COUNTERPOINT

Library of Congress Cataloging-in-Publication Data

Porter, Bill, 1943-
South of the Clouds : travels in southwest China /
Bill Porter.
    pages cm
1. Yunnan Sheng (China)—Description and travel.
2. Porter, Bill, 1943—Travel—China—Yunnan
Sheng. 3. Yunnan Sheng (China)—History, Local.
4. Yunnan Sheng (China)—Social life and customs.
5. Yunnan Sheng (China)—Social conditions.
I. Title.
DS793.Y8P77 2015
951'.35059—dc23

                                            2015009573

ISBN 978-1-61902-719-0

Cover and interior design
by Gopa & Ted2, Inc.

COUNTERPOINT
2560 Ninth Street, Suite 318
Berkeley, CA 94710
www.counterpointpress.com

Printed in the United States of America
Distributed by Publishers Group West

10 9 8 7 6 5 4 3 2 1

Contents

South of the Clouds

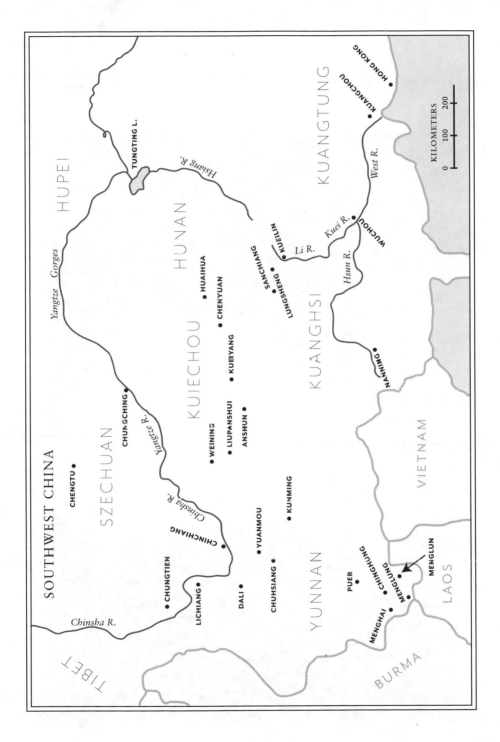

View from Moon Hill

梧州

1. Wuchou

I T WAS MY INTRODUCTION to karma: applying to Columbia University to study for a PhD in anthropology in 1970 and checking all the boxes in the application for financial aid, including a box for a language fellowship, and writing in the word "Chinese" because I had just read Alan Watt's *The Way of Zen* and thought it made wonderful sense, and it had Chinese characters in it. Who would have guessed? And so I ended up collecting a small library of books about the Middle Kingdom. Among my favorites was a historical atlas put together by Chang Ch'i-yun. Chang was one of China's most famous geographers. He was also the first Chinese to receive an advanced degree from Harvard, and at one time he served as the Republic of China's minister of education. When the Nationalists fled to Taiwan in 1949, he joined them. To keep himself busy in his new home, he founded the College of Chinese Culture, where I once spent a semester in academic confinement. It was there, during his annual tea for graduate students, that he introduced me to his atlas and the set of books he wrote spanning fifty centuries of Chinese civilization.

Chang's approach to historical writing was to place events and people in a spatial as well as in a temporal context. It wasn't simply an intellectual conceit. At one time or another, he traveled to every corner of the Chinese empire to provide himself with a better understanding of the stage on which the drama of his country's history took place. Nowadays, historians are lucky if they see the trees outside the library window.

Heading up the West River

In the spring of 1992, I got out Chang's atlas once more, and I noticed that the last area of traditional China to come under Chinese control was the Southwest, the land the Chinese dubbed Yunnan, or South of the Clouds. Ironically, it was the Mongols, not the Chinese, who finally brought that area into the Chinese orbit and opened it up to outsiders as well—outsiders like Marco Polo. As I looked at Chang's map, it didn't take long for the thought to occur to join Marco Polo. And it didn't take long for the thought to become a plan.

The first step was easy. I was living in Hong Kong at the time and bought a ticket on the *Lichiang*. The *Lichiang* left Kowloon every other day from the China Ferry Terminal on Canton Road. She was a twenty-meter-long hovercraft with a seating arrangement like that of an Airbus. I boarded her at seven thirty, and she left right on time at eight o'clock, just as the sun was rising from the godowns at the east end of Hong Kong Harbor.

We headed west—a familiar route. But this time I wasn't headed for Macao and a weekend of gambling at one of Stanley Ho's casinos. Half way to the former Portuguese colony, the *Lichiang* turned north and entered the labyrinth of waterways that made up the Pearl River Delta.

The boat's windows had been clouded by years of exposure to the sea and the sun and were too dull to see anything. But there was room for a few passengers to sit outside on the stern, and I joined them, watching the boat's endless spray as it hung in the morning air. Along the shoreline of banana trees, palms, and sugar cane, village women stopped washing their clothes just long enough to note our passing. Sampans turned their prows toward our wake to keep from being swamped.

An hour later we turned into the West River and began churning upstream to Wuchou, four hundred kilometers and ten hours away. At forty kilometers an hour, the *Lichiang* was fast, considering she was carrying 120 passengers. It was a Hong Kong group. As soon as the island's skyscrapers were out of sight, the mahjong sets appeared, and TV screens began chronicling the latest Cantonese romances and bankruptcies. After I tired of watching the boat's wake, I came back inside and stretched out on a row of empty seats at the back of the cabin. I was just beginning what I expected would be a six-week journey, and I was already feeling tired. I slept all day. The last rays of the setting sun woke me just as we reached our destination.

As far as Chinese towns go, Wuchou wasn't old. It was first built 1,400 years ago, back in the T'ang dynasty, when the Chinese decided they needed a more permanent presence in order to control the trade goods that poured forth from that region—and not only trade goods but people too. While I was standing in line after disembarking, I met the local representative of China Travel. He was waiting for his tour group to clear immigration. I asked him if there was a monument to Emperor Shun in Wuchou. It was as if I had asked him the whereabouts of the moons of Jupiter. He had no idea what I was talking about.

Admittedly, Emperor Shun lived a long time ago, a couple hundred years after the Yellow Emperor. Around 2200 BC Shun led an army into the Southwest to establish Chinese control of trade routes between China and Southeast Asia. During a battle with the tribes in the Wuchou area, Shun was killed, and his body was buried on Chiuyi Mountain— halfway between Wuchou and Hengyang to the north. Hengyang was where Shun had left his two wives. When they heard the news, they both jumped into the Hsiang River and were transformed into its twin spirits. But that was in Hengyang, and I was in Wuchou, where the only talk was talk about trade—trade and tourism.

I wasn't surprised. Wuchou was, after all, the gateway to China's southwestern provinces of Kuanghsi, Kueichou, and Yunnan, and the entrepôt through which all river-borne trade between Southwest China and Kuangchou had to pass. Although Emperor Shun's attempt to gain control of that gateway had been unsuccessful, his descendents eventually succeeded in establishing a town there during the T'ang dynasty, long before Marco Polo's time. The town thrived on trade, and in 1897, as a result of the Burma Convention, Wuchou became one of China's treaty ports and was opened to foreign traders, who came to buy indigo and furs. The town was also the main conduit through which the medicinal herbs and rare animals of Southwest China passed on their way to Kuangchou, Hong Kong, and the rest of the world.

Heading the list of creatures on which the town's trade thrived were snakes. There was an area at the north edge of town where hundreds of thousand of snakes were kept prior to heading down the West River to the kitchens and pharmacies of Kuangchou. But I arrived too late in the day. Even if I had arrived earlier, there wouldn't have been much to see. I was there at the end of February, and snake season was several months away. Still, I wasn't disappointed. Walking down the street north of the riverside hotel where I spent the night, I passed dozens of restaurants with cages full of vipers.

In addition to snake traders, Wuchou also attracted dealers in the more exotic and endangered species of Southwest China. In one restaurant, an eagle paced hunchbacked in a tiny, ridiculous cage. In another cage, a pangolin lay curled into a ball, dreaming its last pangolin dreams and hoping no one would notice it. But someone had. A table of visitors from Kuangchou were discussing its fate with the chef.

While I dined elsewhere on a less exotic plate of fried rice, I considered the route I had outlined for my journey. I planned to travel through the northern tip of Kuanghsi, then west through the provinces of Kueichou and Yunnan. Along the way, I hoped to visit some of the tribes that still clung to their traditional ways of life. At least that was the plan. Twenty years earlier, I had been a student of anthropology, and I was now looking forward to meeting some of the people I had only read about.

I woke up the next morning to the sound of foghorns, as the barges and boats moored below my hotel window began casting off and heading out into the West River. The West River was formed by the confluence of two rivers: the Hsun, which led further west to Kuanghsi's new provincial capital of Nanning, and the Lichiang (or Kueichiang), which led north to the province's old capital of Kueilin. Summer rains lifted the level of both rivers by as much as twenty meters, and summer was the only time of the year that Kueilin could be reached by boat. Since I arrived in late February, I had no choice but to take the daily bus, which left every morning at seven o'clock.

Reluctantly, I climbed aboard. I was still feeling the effects of my ten-hour boat ride and braced myself for the ten-hour bus ride. The road was a narrow two-lane highway, and I expected the worst. But it turned out to be one of the pleasantest ten-hour rides I had ever experienced in China. For the first few hours, the road was lined with eucalyptus and acacia forests and the occasional hillside of cedar or pine. It was also a quiet bus, a bus full of nodding heads. It wasn't until after six hours into the trip that a few of those heads joined me in gawking at what was one of China's most painted and photographed landscapes. Westerners who looked at traditional Chinese paintings usually thought the mountains they portrayed were products of the artist's imagination. Yet there they were: hundreds of baby mountains, mountains that never made it out of childhood. Unlike in the paintings, however, they were naked, picked clean of anything resembling a tree by villagers in search of firewood. Large Chinese characters in white paint covered the rocks at their base, proclaiming them closed for reforestation. Better late than never.

Finally, nine hours after boarding the bus that left Wuchou at daybreak, I got off an hour short of Kueilin in the town of Yangshuo. Since there were still a few hours of daylight left, and since I felt like seeing some of the scenery close-up, I dropped my bag at an old, crumbling place called the Hsilangshan Hotel, rented a bicycle, and pedaled out of town and into the countryside. Eight kilometers and thirty minutes later, I parked my bicycle at the foot of Moon Hill. I was just in time for the sunset.

From the base of the hill, it was a ten-minute hike to the natural arch just below the summit. The arch made the hill look like it had a hole through it in the shape of the moon, hence the name. I walked through the moon, and from the other side I enjoyed one of Yangshuo's most celebrated views: a landscape of tiny mountains in a sea of rivers and rice paddies set off by the last rays of the sun. Two local women were selling souvenirs and soft drinks. After washing away the dust of the trail with an orange soda, I looked through the souvenirs and spotted a copy of Chairman Mao's Little Red Book. It had been issued after the Communist Party's Ninth Plenary in 1969, and in the back was a list of the participants. What caught my attention was that the book's owner had crossed off the names of those who had later been purged. I paid 10RMB for a testament to Lin Piao's last days of glory, and after returning to my bicycle imagined myself pedaling for the Russian border.

陽朔

2. Yangshuo

Y ANGSHUO WASN'T MUCH of a town. It was dwarfed by Kueilin, its more famous cousin an hour to the north. Like Kueilin, it was in the middle of the region of limestone hills that filled every Chinese tourist brochure. After Beijing's Forbidden City and Great Wall and Sian's Underground Army, the karst landscape of Kueilin was the most popular destination among foreign tourists in China. Kueilin, though, was not what it once had been. It was bombed to smithereens by the Japanese during World War II, and was later rebuilt in Great Leap Forward gray cement and white tile. It now featured the standard overpriced tourist facilities and services that catered to large tour groups, which were okay if you didn't mind being treated like a sheep.

Yangshuo, meanwhile, still possessed the charm that Kueilin had lost several decades earlier—assuming it had possessed any charm in the first place. Still, one couldn't expect to be alone in Yangshuo. During the peak season between April and September, tourists and travelers outnumber locals. But that, too, was one of Yangshuo's charms. There were four places in Southwest China where travelers were likely to stay longer than they planned. In that respect, Yangshuo was joined by Hsishuangbanna, Dali, and Lichiang, all of which were in Yunnan, and all of which were on my itinerary, assuming I could get past Kueilin. Another advantage of a stay in Yangshuo was that I didn't have to pay much more than I would for a bowl of noodles for a banana pancake and a cappuccino, both on the menu the next morning at a place called Mickey Mao's.

With such a delightful beginning to my day, I wondered what would be next. There was a lot to see. I began a few blocks away at the river that flowed past Yangshuo. It was the Lichiang. A cruise along its glassy water was the most popular river cruise in China, more popular even than a cruise through the Yangtze Gorges. The reason for its popularity was the landscape. Between Kueilin and Yangshuo the Lichiang wound past hundreds of tree-covered limestone hills (unlike the denuded ones to the south). If the river was high enough, which it was during the summer, visitors boarded tour boats in Kueilin, cruised downriver to Yangshuo, then returned to Kueilin by bus. But the charge for the six-hour trip was steep. It was 30 bucks during my visit in the spring of 1992, which was one more reason to stay in Yangshuo instead of Kueilin.

From Yangshuo, there was a boat that left every morning heading upriver, and it cost a mere 6 dollars. It only went halfway, but for most people halfway was enough. I decided to avoid the cruise business altogether and to strike out on my own. Anytime I traveled without a crowd, it was more of an adventure. And when I got home, it was the adventures I remembered.

Once again I rented a bicycle at my hotel and pedaled back to Yangshuo's riverside park. For less than 3 dollars, I hired a flat-bottomed boat to take me downriver to the village of Fuli, from which I could then pedal back to Yangshuo through the countryside. It took about an hour to make the six-kilometer journey downriver. The river was as smooth as glass. And on the way, I saw the same sort of limestone crags people saw in their big tour boats upriver. But I was alone, or nearly alone. I shared the river with the occasional fisherman steering his long, narrow bamboo raft through eelgrass in search of deeper water where his cormorants could dive for fish.

The man poling me downriver said the fishermen also fished on the river at night by torchlight. He said they raised their cormorants as chicks and taught them to chase live fish with a string tied around their leg to prevent them from escaping. When they were big and docile enough, they joined a half dozen other cormorants on the gunwale of the fisherman's boat and took turns diving for fish at the fisherman's

The Lichiang near Yangshuo

command. But there was now a string around the bird's neck to prevent it from swallowing its prey. According to my boatman, after about five years of this, the birds became increasingly unwilling to dive for fish they weren't allowed to eat—as if it took them five years to figure this out—and they ended up as cormorant stew.

On the way downriver, I spotted a lone kingfisher perched on a snag along the shore. There was no string around its neck, and I couldn't help but wonder whether I was a cormorant or a kingfisher.

桂林

3. Kueilin

AFTER PEDALING BACK to Yangshuo, I returned the bicycle, checked out of my hotel, and caught the next bus heading north. I would have preferred to avoid the tourist trap of Kueilin altogether, but I couldn't avoid its bus station. I arrived just after twelve and bought a ticket on the afternoon bus to the mountain town of Lungsheng, where I hoped to visit some of the hill tribes in the province. Since I had a few hours to kill, I thought I might as well see a few of the sights. Just outside the bus station, I caught a local bus and got off where a limestone hill shaped like an elephant was extending its trunk into the Lichiang River.

The story went like this: a long time ago, a herd of elephants wandered into the Kueilin area to eat the bananas that grew there. When the villagers saw the elephants, they thought about how much less work they would have to do if they could tame the beasts. After several fatal attempts, they finally succeeded. When the emperor of China heard about this, he ordered the villagers to bring the elephants to the capital so that he could use them in his army.

When the villagers refused, the emperor wasn't pleased, and he led his army to Kueilin and killed all the people he could find. In celebration of his victory, the emperor mounted the biggest of the elephants. But as soon as he climbed on top, the elephant tried to throw him off. In desperation, the emperor sank his sword into the elephant's back. But this only made the elephant madder, and it threw the emperor to the ground

Reed Flute Cave

and trampled him to death. When the emperor was sufficiently flat, the king of the jungle walked down to the river to quench its thirst, and it has been there drinking the Lichiang's water ever since. The emperor's sword was still sticking out of its back, although the weapon had since turned into a pagoda.

In addition to Elephant Trunk and its other karst hills, Kueilin was also home to some of Southwest China's most famous underground scenery. I reboarded the same bus, changed to another one, and thirty minutes later got off at the entrance of Reed Flute Cave. I was just in time for the hourly tour and joined five other visitors. One travel book compared this series of caverns to the set used for the movie *Journey to the Center of the Earth*. It wasn't a bad comparison. I confess, I enjoyed every minute, all thirty of them, which was how long the tour lasted. As we walked through the various caverns, our guide pointed out the sights and told us what we should be seeing. One cavern was full of animals, another was full of vegetables, another was full of gods and buddhas, another was a forest of mushrooms. I wondered what people were supposed to see during the Cultural Revolution: paper tigers, I suppose.

Thirty minutes was just right. Afterwards, I headed back into town on yet another bus. This time I got off at West Hill Park. The hill once included over two hundred buddha statues carved out of its cliffs 1,200 years ago. Unfortunately, most of the carvings had been destroyed or damaged during the Cultural Revolution, and the attempt to replace them with cement replicas was not very satisfying.

I directed my attention, instead, to the Kueilin Museum just inside the park entrance. The museum was built on the site of what used to be a Buddhist temple. As I walked inside, I passed display cases containing the remains of some of Kueilin's early residents, including several human teeth that someone had left behind in a cave thirty thousand years ago. Next was an exhibit that recreated the burial of a body tied up in the fetal position and placed inside a large pottery urn. It was a realistic display and even included several women wailing and a child cringing behind one of the women. They were all wearing animal skins. I wondered why the museum didn't promote the city's cloth. Kueilin was once famous for its cotton and hemp fabrics. The T'ang dynasty poet Pai Chu-yi once wrote: "Kueilin cloth is white as snow / Suchou silk is soft as a cloud / Kueilin cloth weighs more than silk / but a Kueilin robe will keep you warmer."

The museum also included a three-meter-high rubbing from the Sung dynasty. It was a map of Kueilin, and was one of the oldest, largest, and most detailed maps of an ancient Chinese city I had ever seen. The stone stele from which it was copied was carved in the year 1279. Just past the map, I entered a hall devoted to the tribal peoples that still lived in the province's more mountainous areas to the north. Filling the hall were a dozen bronze drums, most of them a thousand or more years old. I had never seen drums that big, and I tried to imagine how members of the region's hill tribes had made them—or why. There were no explanations, so I moved on to the final wing, where the clothing displays were the best I saw anywhere in Southwest China. Instead of putting each tribe's distinctive handmade clothing in display cases or on mannequins, the curator put it on well-crafted statues of people singing and dancing and playing musical instruments. And the exhibits were up to date. Most of the men, for example, wore olive drab army tennis shoes.

China's ethnic minorities were the reason for my trip, and I was anxious to see real people, not dioramas. I paused just long enough in the museum store to buy a book about the province's hill tribes, then headed back out to the street. There was one other sight I had hoped to visit, but it was two hours northeast of Kueilin. It was one of China's greatest and oldest hydraulic achievements. The year was 221 BC, and the megalomaniac known to the world as the First Emperor had just crushed the last of the kingdoms into which China had been divided since prehistoric times. To maintain his grip on his far-flung territories, the First Emperor ordered construction of a wall to keep out invaders from the north and a canal to supply his forces stationed in the south.

The emperor sent three of his generals to the mountains northeast of Kueilin to oversee construction of a thirty-kilometer-long canal that linked the Hsiang River with the Lichiang. It was a brilliant conception. Linking the two rivers allowed boats to travel from the Yangtze River via Tungting Lake and the Hsiang River to the West River and all the way to the South China Sea. Equally remarkable was that the system remained in use until modern times. The huge block of masonry used to divert water into the canal was reportedly still there, as were the locks added later. Also, nearby were the tombs of the three generals who had supervised construction. Apparently, they didn't finish on schedule. I, too, was out of time. Instead of waiting for the next bus, I flagged down a taxi. It was a good thing I did. I got to the station with only five minutes to spare and left to see an even more amazing man-made wonder.

壮族

4. The Chuang

THE OFFICIAL NAME of Kuanghsi province is the Kuanghsi Chuang
Autonomous Region. Next to the Han Chinese, the Chuang are
China's largest ethnic group. That surprises people. Most people would
think it was the Manchus, or the Uigurs, or the Mongols, or the Tibetans. But in 1990 there were 15 million Chuang in China, compared to
10 million Manchus, 7 million Uigurs, 5 million Mongols, and 4.5 million Tibetans. Since most of China's 15 million Chuang live in Kuanghsi,
hence the province's distinction as the Kuanghsi Chuang Autonomous
Region.

Unlike China's other ethnic minorities, the Chuang and their ancestors
have lived where they are living now since prehistoric times. According
to historians, they were responsible for the country's oldest rock paintings, a few kilometers from the country's border with Vietnam. Many
of the paintings date back more than 2,500 years. In those days the
Han Chinese referred to all the tribes south of their control as Yueh, or
Outsiders. The term "Chuang," which the Chuang use in referring to
themselves, wasn't used by the Han Chinese until 1,000 years ago. Of
course, as with all tribes, Chuang history or prehistory goes back more
than 2,500 years, all the way back to the beginning of time.

According to the Chuang, in the beginning there was a big ball of
swirling energy covered by a hard shell, and one day a big bee came
along. Don't ask where the bee came from, it just came along. And
the bee punctured the shell. When it did, gas escaped to form the sky

Carving of an ancestor on a Chuang grave

above, water rained down to form the rivers and the seas, and earth fell into the rivers and seas to form the mountains and plains. And plants grew on the earth, and they gave rise to flowers, and from one of the flowers a woman appeared with long, flowing hair, wearing no clothes. Her name was Mu Liu-chia. She had been asleep a long time, and the first thing she did was pee. Then, to amuse herself, she mixed her pee with mud and made human beings. It was a big mistake. But Mu Liu-chia just laughed. Then, to differentiate between men and women, she gathered some red peppers and carambola fruits and scattered them on the ground. The humans who picked up red peppers became men, while those who grabbed carambola fruits became women. And if you are ever in a Chuang village, you want to be careful when referring to red peppers and carambola (also known as star) fruits, because the terms have been used ever since to make jokes about human genitalia.

The reason I was able to read this creation story was that despite the steady migration of Han Chinese into Kuanghsi, China's largest ethnic minority had maintained its cultural identity, and Chinese anthropologists had recorded its myths. Although most Chuang now lived in cities and towns, they could still recite these stories, and there were still tens of thousands of Chuang who lived as their ancestors did in remote mountain villages—one of which was my destination. After three hours of weaving its way through the mountains north of Kueilin, the bus I was on dropped me off in the village of Hoping. I was headed for a Chuang village, but Hoping wasn't it. I had to wait for the minibus that passed through Hoping every hour or so on its way up a side valley to Shuang-hokou, or Twin Rivers.

While I waited for my bus, I sat down on my backpack at the side of the road and continued reading the story about the origin of the Chuang in the book I had bought earlier at the Kueilin Museum. After Mu Liu-chia made humans out of urine and mud, she disappeared, and the scene shifted to a cave from which four brothers appeared. The eldest was Thunder, and he was followed by Dragon and Tiger and finally Pu Lo-t'uo, who was the ancestor of the Chuang people.

Huanglo bridge

Thunder, Dragon, and Tiger made fun of Pu Lo-t'uo, because he didn't have any special powers like they did. Then one day Pu Lo-t'uo discovered fire, and he ran to show his older brothers. When he did, his brothers were so terrified, Thunder flew into the clouds, Dragon dove into the river, and Tiger ran into the forest. Ever since then, Pu Lo-t'uo's descendants have been safe from his mischievous older brothers. Well, more or less safe. The Chuang are still careful to offer sacrifices so that Thunder sends down rain for their crops, and Dragon keeps their springs flowing, and Tiger keeps them from harm when they enter the forest.

Just as I finished the story about Pu Lo-t'uo, the minibus arrived. It was a twelve-seat van, and I squeezed in with thirty other passengers, all of them Chuang villagers heading home after market day in Lungsheng. Thirty minutes later, I got out at a bump in the road called Huanglo. According to the bus driver, the trail to the village where I hoped to spend the night began on the other side of the river where he dropped me off. And it was a raging river, full of tree branches and logs. According to the driver, it had been raining for twenty days, and I was lucky to

Covered bridge near Pingan

be arriving with the sun, which looked to be about an hour away from disappearing behind the ridge across the river.

Unfortunately, the only way across was on a wooden bridge that looked to be about a foot and a half wide. After watching several village children skip across on its log planks, I tried, if only out of embarrassment. It was a good thing I had a walking stick to help me keep my balance. It saved me several times. Once across, I walked over to the children who had been watching to see if I would fall and asked for directions to the village of Pingan. They all pointed to a trail that began behind the village. I waved goodbye and started up.

The trail was fairly steep and still slick from the recent rains, but my walking stick came to the rescue, and more than once. After about half an hour I passed a grove of tea trees. Normally tea trees were kept short to make it easier to pick the leaves. But these were several meters high. I found out later that they were being cultivated not for their leaves, but for their fruit, which the Chuang used to make cooking oil.

After another half hour, I arrived at a covered bridge. I was getting close, which was good, because the last rays of the sun were slipping behind the ridge to the west. Nearly all the mountain tribes in that part of China build a covered bridge to let outsiders know when they're approaching their village. Sure enough, around the next bend a dozen wooden houses came into view, and I met several villagers walking toward me going down the same trail. They smiled and said, "Meng-ni-o," which means "hello."

And so I arrived at Pingan. Pingan was just below the ridge of a mountain that had the highest concentration of rice terraces in China. Some of the terraces were so narrow, they only had space for one row of rice plants. And they extended eight hundred meters almost straight up from the bottom of the valley where I got off the bus, all the way to the top of the ridge. Work on these terraces began five hundred years ago, when the Chuang were forced out of the Kueilin plains by migrations of Han Chinese from the north. I arrived in late February, and the terraces were being flooded in preparation for spring planting, which was still several months away.

When I entered the village, I heard a chorus of meng-ni-o's, as heads and whole bodies appeared in doorways. Although the Chuang and their ancestors had been living in this part of China for at least three thousand years, they had never developed a written language of their own. Fortunately, many of their songs and stories had been recorded during the past two thousand years using Chinese-style characters that indicated the meaning as well as the sound of Chuang words. As a result, the Chuang had retained more of their traditional mythology than most of China's other ethnic minorities.

As I followed the trail past their houses, villagers gathered around me and led me into the only level place in the village: the basketball court. A few minutes later, the village headman appeared and led me to his house. As I climbed the stairs to the second floor and stepped inside, his wife began blowing on embers in the fire pit in the middle of a room that took up half the second floor. I sat down on a six-inch-high wooden stool next to the fire pit, and the woman's husband poured me a bowl of the finest rice wine I had ever tasted. Meanwhile, he singed the hair off a pig's foot, and his wife sliced some fresh bamboo shoots and started making a soup. Dinner, I could tell, was going to be memorable.

Chuang houses are two-storey affairs, with the animals and tools and firewood and latrine underneath and the people above on the second floor. All the cooking takes place in and around the fire pit in the middle of the main room. The pit is filled with sand and lined with rock, and there are always a few embers in the ashes just waiting for mealtime or for a guest to arrive. And hanging above the fire pit, there's a frame for smoking meat and for keeping stuff dry.

The headman's wife reached up and grabbed a sausage and cut off a couple inches. Then, to let me know I was getting the whole hog, she lifted the lid of a crock, ladled out a couple dippers of pig's blood, and poured the liquid into the soup. This was really going to be good. Then, to spice things up, she took out some scissors and cut a few chunks off a bunch of dried peppers. Suddenly I remembered the Chuang association of red peppers with male genitalia and winced. It was a great meal, I think. All I really remember is that my host never stopped filling my bowl with rice wine, which he said he'd aged for a whole week. The next morning I woke up without my shoes or clothes and no memory of having taken them off. Apparently, I had a good time.

I could have slept until noon, but the village forge was right below my window, and the blacksmith started work early. Being awake was painful, but I couldn't go back to sleep. I said a reluctant hello to my first rice wine hangover. Finally, when the sun was high enough to make it over the ridge, my host came in and asked me if I needed a toothbrush. The one he offered me looked like it had been used by the whole village. My host's name was Mr. Liao. Pingan's rice terraces attracted photographers from as far away as Beijing, Shanghai, and Hong Kong, but I arrived in late February, when all people did was drink rice wine and chew pork fat and talk about the fine harvest they were going to have. With the surge of outside interest in the village's man-made wonder, my host had been quick to realize the potential for profit. Ten years earlier he'd persuaded the local government to declare his home a hostel in order to accommodate visitors.

The village of Pingan

Rice terraces of Pingan

Author's Chuang host and her sister

I turned down the toothbrush, and after locating my clothes and shoes stumbled back to the fire pit. I was just in time for breakfast, which was pretty much leftover dinner. And once more my bowl was filled with rice wine. The Chuang like to say that they never let a guest leave sober, and in my case, they maintained their ancient tradition unblemished. While they heated up the leftovers, the wife and her sister took turns singing. Afterwards, the sister invited me to her village on the other side of the ridge. But I had other plans, and after breakfast I said, "Huai-p'ai-ao," which means "goodbye" in the Chuang language, and I staggered down the mountain and back to the road that had brought me there.

While I waited for the local minibus, I tried to recall some of the stories I had heard before the night became a blur. The only one I could remember had to do with frogs. The Chuang consider frogs sacred creatures, because frogs are the children of Thunder. When the Chuang are in need of rain, all they have to do is tell the frogs, and the frogs tell Thunder. According to the story I had heard the previous night, a long time ago an old woman couldn't sleep because of the croaking of frogs outside her window, and she asked her son to make them stop. Her son's name was Tung Lin-lang, and his solution was to pour boiling water outside the second-floor windows. It worked, and the frogs that weren't scalded to death hopped away. And they kept hopping, and all the other frogs joined them. Soon there were no more frogs left on the mountain. And when summer came, there was no rain, only the scorching heat of the sun.

In desperation, Tung Lin-lang went to the village shrine and asked Pu Lo-t'uo what to do. Pu Lo-t'uo, you might remember, was the ancestor of the Chuang. He told Tung Lin-lang that the frogs he had killed were the children of Thunder, and unless he asked Thunder for forgiveness and henceforth treated frogs as members of his own family, there would be no more rain. Well, Tung Lin-lang did as he was told, and ever since then, the frog festival has been the biggest Chuang festival of the year.

The festival begins on the first day of the lunar new year. As soon as the village elders see the sun, they beat the village's bronze drum. Chuang drums, like the ones I saw in the Kueilin Museum, are huge and made of bronze. Historians aren't sure why the Chuang went to so much trouble to make these drums. It wasn't cheap or easy to make a bronze drum. But if you ask me, it all came down to the Chuang belief that frogs are the children of Thunder, and that without their intercession there would be no rain for their rice. The drums were meant to imitate Thunder's voice. In any case, once the drum sounds on the morning of New Year's Day, everyone gathers in the village square, which when I visited was the basketball court in front of the village school. Everyone brings hoes and other farm tools, and after praying for good luck, they head off to the surrounding hillsides to find a frog. They turn over rocks and dig beside streams and ponds, and the first man and the first woman who find a frog bring their frogs back to the village and become the frog king and the frog queen. They then give their frogs to the village shaman, who recounts all the stories about frogs and how important they are as messengers of Thunder. Then the shaman kills the frogs and puts them in a bamboo coffin and places the coffin in the village shrine, and the party begins. And it begins again every night for two weeks until the first full moon, when the frogs go to Heaven to tell Thunder to send down rain, and everything is okay in the Chuang world for another year. As I sat there at the side of the road, I was surprised I remembered all this and yet didn't remember taking off my shoes and clothes the night before.

Chuang house in Pingan

瑤族

5. The Yao

THIS TIME WHEN the minibus showed up, there was plenty of room. I even had a seat. And the hangover was gone. But by the time the bus reached Lungsheng, there was barely room to breathe. It was another market day. That was why Lungsheng was there. It was a mountain market that had finally made up its mind to become a town. There were even a couple of places that called themselves hotels. But first impressions count for a lot, and as soon as I arrived, I was anxious to leave. I walked across the bridge to the new part of town, and next to the Lungsheng Gymnasium, I caught the last bus of the day to a hot spring near the village of Chiangti.

While the bus wound its way up a long valley to the northeast, half a dozen passengers invited me to their home for the night. They were all mountain people going back to their villages after a big day in Lungsheng. Some came to buy, and some came to sell. They were all Yao. Unlike Chuang women, who wore pretty much all black, with just a single band of dark-blue embroidery around their elbows and knees, Yao women wore jackets completely covered with embroidery. Those whose embroidery was done with red or pink thread called themselves Red Yao. Others identified with a place or a myth.

The lady sitting next to me was a P'an Yao, P'an being short for P'an-ku, the ancestor of the Yao people. When I told her I was from America, she said some Chinese anthropologists had come to her village a few years earlier and told them they spoke the same kind of language

The trail to Ailing

as some tribe in America. When I told her I was part Cherokee and that we might be related, she looked at me and laughed.

Just before the bus reached the village of Chiangti, I got off and waved goodbye to her and all the other passengers who had invited me to their home for the night. I opted instead for the Wenshui hot spring, which was a ten-minute walk down a muddy road. Judging from the ruts, business was good.

As soon as I had checked in at the one and only hotel and dropped my bag in my room, I headed for the pools. The hot spring consisted of three huge pools set against a cliff and flanked on either side by forest. It was a beautiful setting, and I was anxious to become part of it. Unfortunately, all three pools were in the open, and bathers were required to wear swimsuits. Since I didn't have a swimsuit, I had to buy one. And the only kind for sale was of the one-size-fits-all variety. No problem, I thought, and went to change. Apparently I had put on some weight, and the seams strained to contain my bulk. As I emerged, a pair of Chinese bathers took one look and said to each other, "Wow, look at that guy. He's so fat." I was in shock. I had always considered myself

Village bridge near Ailing

a modest-sized individual, and now I was having trouble wearing the one-size-fits-all swimsuit. I remembered weighing myself a week earlier in Hong Kong. The little card that had fallen out of the slot above the scale had said 190 pounds. Now I was being confronted by the hard truth of what 190 pounds meant for someone five feet seven inches tall. I slipped into the pool, hid beneath the steaming water, and considered my options. Obviously, I was living too large. As a feeble gesture, I decided that for the rest of this trip I was going to limit myself to one beer every other day. I had to do something.

Later that night while I was dining on noodles and enjoying a solitary every-other-day beer, the girl who had sold me the swimsuit and who also worked in the hotel restaurant told me about a Yao village in the nearby mountains. The name of the village was Ailing. She said it could only be reached by walking eight kilometers along a trail that skirted the side of the valley behind the hot spring. She said it was one of the few traditional Yao villages left in that area.

There were two million Yao in China, and nearly half of them lived in the province of Kuanghsi. Unlike the ancestors of the Chuang, who were already there 2,500 years ago, the ancestors of the Yao lived along the lower reaches of the Yangtze. According to the Yao, they lived in a kingdom ruled by King P'ing, which was repeatedly invaded by a kingdom to the north ruled by King Kao. Historians think this occurred during the Chou dynasty about 2,700 years ago.

Frustrated by the constant attacks, King P'ing promised to marry his daughter to anyone who could kill King Kao. Among King P'ing's prize possessions was a dragon-dog named P'an-hu, and when P'an-hu overheard his master's promise, he crossed the Yangtze, and seven days later arrived at the palace of King Kao. Since he was only a dog, no one paid any attention until it was too late. P'an-hu rushed into the king's bedchamber and bit off the king's head and brought it back to King P'ing.

Well, a promise is a promise, so the king gave P'an-hu his daughter in marriage. Strangely enough, the princess fell in love with P'an-hu. Still, she wasn't completely happy. She told her father that her husband turned into a handsome man in a fur robe at night, but that in the morning he turned back into a dog. What to do?

P'an-hu was rather enjoying the best of both worlds, but when the princess implored him to become a man for good, he agreed. The royal shaman placed P'an-hu in a covered cage and hung him over a boiling cauldron. According to the shaman, after seven days of steaming with medicinal plants, P'an-hu would turn into a man for good. But after six days, the princess could wait no longer. She ordered her husband removed from the cage. To her delight, not only was he still alive, he was no longer a dog. But because he was taken down early, he still had patches of dog hair on his head and between his legs. To keep her father from finding out that P'an-hu was still part dog, the princess covered her husband's hirsute parts with a turban and pants, which ever since then have been the traditional dress of Yao men. Meanwhile, her father was overjoyed, and his son-in-law succeeded him as king of the region around the modern city of Nanking. In the years that followed, King P'an-hu and his queen had twelve children, and years later, when the kingdom was overrun by the Han Chinese, his descendents migrated south to Kuanghsi, where they still live, children of the dragon-dog.

And so the next morning, I set out for the dragon-dog village of Ailing. The trail was easy, and it was shaded by heavy forest and cooled by mountain streams. Along the way, I met several Yao women on their way to town with large plastic containers to buy kerosene. Kerosene was one of the few things the Yao weren't able to produce themselves. Further on, I passed a couple of Yao men resting on a log. Each of them had an ancient, single-shot flintlock rifle. They said they were going bear hunting. The bears in those mountains must be small, I thought. Usually the first shot only makes a bear mad. More likely, they didn't intend to shoot bears, just look for signs. The Yao have always relied on hunting to augment their normal diet of rice and pork, but they have developed their own hunting style. When someone finds traces of a mountain sheep or a wild pig, or a bear, they go back to the village for help. The villagers then surround the area where the animal was last sighted, and they beat drums and drive the animal toward other villagers armed with rifles and hunting bows. At least, that is how they hunt for mountain sheep and wild pigs. Maybe it's different for bears.

I wished the hunters luck and continued on. Less than two hours after setting out, I finally reached the telltale sign that a mountain village was near: a covered bridge. Sure enough, a few minutes later, I entered the village of Ailing. A couple of village dogs barked the ancestral Yao greeting, and I barked back.

As I followed the dirt trail into Ailing, the only signs I could see that its Yao residents had met the twentieth century were plastic kerosene containers outside the doorways. Still, the nearest road was only eight kilometers away, and villagers could travel to Lungsheng to sell their produce and buy necessities and make it back the same day. So they weren't completely cut off from the modern world. But as I walked through their village, they all looked utterly astounded to see a Westerner. In fact, some of them looked terrified. Finally, a group of young men overcame their fright and emerged from a doorway to ask what I was doing. After telling them I had come with no other purpose than to visit, I asked them what they were doing. They said they were preparing for an initiation ceremony.

In order for a Yao male to be considered a man, he had to undergo three days of fasting in total darkness together with all the other would-be men in the village. Then, after three days of no light, no food, and no sleep, he had to perform certain feats, the last of which was to jump from a three-meter-high platform. If he could land without falling down, he became a man. If not, he had to try again the following year. Apparently, the boys of Ailing were about to try again.

After this initial exchange, the boys returned to the dark interior of the stilt house they were occupying. Less than a minute later, they came back out holding trade goods. It was a strange reception. Apparently, the appearance of a Westerner in their village was so startling, they forgot their traditional hospitality. Instead of inviting me in for the customary bowl of fried tea, they brought out stuff for me to buy. I was being viewed not as a guest, but as a merchant from afar. Still, it was an instructive experience. One of the boys preparing for his initiation even offered to sell me two small lumps of gold he had dug out of the nearby hills. I passed.

Meanwhile, several village women came out onto the balcony of the house next door to see what was happening. They were all wearing traditional Yao jackets covered on the front and back and even on the sleeves with pink embroidery. They looked like cherry trees in bloom, and I complimented them on their clothing. But no sooner were the words out of my mouth, than they asked me if I wanted to buy their jackets.

Yao embroidery was the finest of that of any tribe in China. It took a woman at least a year of her spare time to embroider a single jacket. One of the women led me into her house and showed me the loom where she wove the cloth and the basket full of colored thread that would become part of her next jacket. I ended up buying the jacket she was wearing for 200RMB, or 40 dollars. It was a lot of money for them as well as for me, but I had never seen such beautiful embroidery and so much of it on a single piece of clothing.

Obviously I was a merchant now. The next thing I knew, the women

A Yao woman working at her loom

were offering me not only their jackets and skirts, but even their hair, long braids of silken tresses. I never got around to asking the price, because I wasn't in the market for hair. The women told me they cut their hair every ten years, then washed it and combed it out and rubbed it with perfumed oil and coiled it on top of their head. They said that this allowed them to change their hair every three or four days.

I must have spent an hour inspecting all the merchandise they brought out for me to look at. But except for buying the jacket, I just smiled and thanked them for showing me their prized possessions. I think the villagers of Ailing were somewhat disappointed. For my part, I was also disappointed, disappointed that I wasn't treated as a normal guest and wasn't even offered the traditional fried tea, which the Yao make by frying tea leaves, soybeans, corn, peanuts, and puffed rice, to which they then add boiling water and scallion tops and pepper. Guests are supposed to drink four bowls, and I wasn't offered even one.

I slipped out of the village as quietly as I had entered, and I think that was my problem. A few minutes later as I approached the bridge I had crossed earlier, I met an old man on his way back to Ailing who invited me to spend the night. Suddenly I realized the reason for the strange reception I had received earlier. Visitors aren't supposed to enter a mountain village without being invited. They're supposed to stop somewhere on the trail near the village and wait. That was the purpose of the covered bridge. When I asked the old man which house I could stay at, he said, "Any house, take your pick. But first come to my house for some tea."

And so I followed him back into the village, and he led me up the wooden stairs into the second floor of his house, where I finally tasted some fried tea. Ailing was one of the larger Yao villages in China. According to my host, eighty families, or more than five hundred people, lived in Ailing, and each family had its own two-storey wooden house. As with the Chuang houses I had seen earlier in Pingan, the first storey was used for storing things like firewood and tools, the family latrine, and stalls for cattle and pigs. The second storey contained the living quarters and the family hearth, and was also used for household industries, like turning soybeans into tofu or trees into lumber. For such purposes, the second storey included plenty of open space.

On my way into Ailing, I had noticed a new house going up, and I asked my host how much it cost to build something like that. He said it cost 10,000RMB, or the equivalent of 2,000 dollars. The money, he said, was for thanking fellow villagers for their assistance in turning local fir trees into beams and boards and for their help in house construction. He said Yao houses were expected to last 150 years, or five generations. The old man said he and his ancestors had been living in Ailing a long time. In some Yao villages, archaeologists have found coins dating back to the T'ang dynasty, or 1,200 years ago.

By the time I had finished the obligatory four bowls of fried tea, I heard the wind beginning to pick up outside and decided it was time to leave. I thanked my host for his hospitality and also for his invitation to spend the night. But I felt the pull of the hot spring and headed back the way I had come. Halfway there, the rain caught up with me. But it wasn't a heavy rain. I just walked faster, and before long I was soaking again and wondering why the Yao didn't build their village closer to the steaming waters. Then again, maybe they did, long ago.

Tung drum tower

侗族

6. The Tung

I COULD HAVE SOAKED for days, but I wasn't meant to soak for days. It was only afternoon, and this wasn't a vacation. I went back to my room and collected my gear and checked out. On my way out of the hotel, I stopped to thank the girl who had told me about the village of Ailing. I showed her the jacket I had bought. She said I should have bought hers. I probably would have, but I hadn't seen her wearing it. All I had seen was a Western-style vest with the hotel's name and a hot spring logo on it. I waved goodbye and walked back down the muddy ruts that served as the road. Ten minutes later, I was standing at the side of the paved highway, and five minutes after that I was on a bus bound for Lungsheng, where I arrived just in time to catch the last bus of the day to my next destination, the town of Sanchiang.

Once again, I was traveling with a bus full of villagers heading back to the hills after a day at the market. Halfway to Sanchiang, a man got on with an old flintlock rifle. He said he'd been hunting wild pigs. He said they sometimes got as big as 200 kilos. I know I wouldn't want to hunt an animal that big and that dangerous with a single-shot flintlock. Maybe the man was a good shot. Or maybe he shot from the safety of a tree.

Finally, two hours after leaving Lungsheng and about an hour after the sun went down, I arrived in Sanchiang. I passed up the bus station hotel and walked up the hill behind the station parking lot to the government hostel. It was clean and quiet, and a room with my own bathroom and hot water only cost 18RMB, or less than 4 dollars. It was a far cry from the tourist traps of Kueilin. After washing my clothes and taking a shower, I headed back down the hill to the one street that ran through town. It was lined with dog-meat restaurants. Obviously, Sanchiang was not Yao territory. The Yao were descendants of P'an-hu, the dragon-dog, and they ate everything except dog meat. Sanchiang, it turned out, was home to the Tung. I opted, instead, for a plate of fried dumplings and called it a night. Later, back in my room, I heard a group of Tung girls singing somewhere in the distance. It sounded just like the Hopi rain chant I once learned when I was a student of anthropology. Sure enough, later that night it poured.

In 1990, the government counted 2.5 million Tung living in the Southwest. Unlike the Chuang, whose ancestors had lived in this area as early as 2,500 years ago, or the Yao, who migrated here over 1,000 years ago, the Tung were recent arrivals. According to linguists, the Tung language preserved a number of features of the Chinese language as it was spoken 700 years ago. During that period, there was a huge influx of Han Chinese into the middle reaches of the Yangtze, which was the ancestral homeland of the Tung. As a result, the Tung were pushed south and ended up in the mountains of Hunan, Kueichou, and Kuanghsi. It was also about that time that the Chinese first mentioned the Tung in their historical records. The Tung, though, didn't call themselves Tung. They called themselves Kan. In the Tung language, "kan" means "tree stump," and it turns out that the Tung and tree stumps are related.

According to the Tung account of their origins, once upon a time a tree stump gave birth to a fungus. And the fungus gave birth to a mushroom. And the mushroom gave birth to a rivulet. And the rivulet gave birth to a crayfish. And the crayfish gave birth to E-jung. And E-jung gave birth to Ch'i-chieh. And Ch'i-chieh gave birth to a girl named Sung-sang and a boy named Sung-en. Sung-sang and Sung-en had twelve children, and among them were Thunder, Dragon, Snake, Bear, Tiger, and the parents of the Tung people: Chiang-liang and Chiang-mei. Because Chiang-liang and Chiang-mei didn't care for their brothers and sisters, they decided to chase them away, which they did by setting fire to the mountain where they all lived together. Ever since then, the Tung have lived apart from their animal kin, which explains why they prefer to build their villages in valley bottoms instead of on the higher slopes. It also makes visiting a Tung village a lot easier than visiting a Yao village, which was what I did the next morning.

I boarded the first bus of the day to Linchi. Linchi was forty kilometers northeast of Sanchiang, but I wasn't going that far. Halfway there, the bus dropped me off at a bridge that led to the Tung village of Chengyang. I stared in disbelief. When the Tung began migrating to this part of China, they brought with them a skill in woodworking superior to that of any other tribe. One look at the bridge that spanned the Linchi River, and it was obvious that the Tung are right when they say they're descended from trees, or at least the stumps of trees.

Over the previous few days, I had noticed the custom among the people living in that part of China of building covered bridges near their villages. The bridges not only improved access and eliminated certain dangers of the trail but also represented a village's face to outsiders, and villages tried to outdo each other in building bigger and more ornate

Tung bridge at village of Chengyang

structures. In that respect, the villagers of Chengyang had outdone everyone.

They built this particular bridge in 1906 to replace an earlier one. It only took them a year to finish the basic structure, but they spent the next ten elaborating it into one of the most amazing pieces of architecture anywhere in China. The bridge was slightly damaged during the Cultural Revolution, but since then it had been placed under state protection and the damage repaired.

In terms of its dimensions, the Chengyang Bridge was 75 meters long and 3.5 meters wide. Along the sides, more than a hundred wooden posts supported a tiled roof punctuated by five multi-storey pavilions. The whole structure looked like a series of temples strung across the river on granite pylons. In addition to its unique form, the bridge was also noteworthy for the absence of a single nail. Everything was held together by mortise-and-tenon construction: a mortise being a rectangular slot carved into the end of a beam, and a tenon being a rectangular projection from another beam that fit into the adjacent mortise.

I walked across, listening to the bridge's mortises and tenons creak like a pond full of frogs. Once across, I followed a dirt path into the village of Chengyang. The path to every Tung village was traditionally paved with stones so that visitors wouldn't have to walk in the mud. Apparently times had changed in Chengyang. It had rained the night before, and I entered the village with part of the path on my shoes. Still, Chengyang had preserved the most important feature of any Tung village: its drum tower.

It was four or five meters high and consisted of a series of seven roofs with their corners upturned, and with each roof being successively smaller. On top of the highest roof was a small pagoda. The architecture looked like it had been inspired by the temples of Cambodia or Thailand, but maybe that was just my imagination.

A villager I had met earlier on the bus saw me gawking at the structure and led me inside. Except for benches around the walls, the tower was empty. The log drum that normally would have hung from the upper rafters was also missing. Apparently, it had been replaced by some other means of communication, but I couldn't see any loudspeakers. Tung villages traditionally used log drums to call village meetings, and the drum tower was where village elders met to discuss village affairs.

Outside, in front of the drum tower, was an open area, where village festivals were held. And next to the open area was the village shrine, where the most important rituals took place. It was the shrine to the great heroine of the Tung people. Outsiders weren't allowed inside, but my guide was kind enough to tell me her story.

Her name was Sa-sui. Every Tung village had a shrine to her, he said, and Chengyang was no exception. No one knew when Sa-sui lived, only that she lived a long time ago. In the Tung language, "sa" means "grandmother" or "matriarch," and "sui" means "first." But Sa-sui wasn't the first ancestor of the Tung people. That honor belongs to Chiang-liang and Chiang-mei, the Tung Adam and Eve. Sa-sui was their Moses.

In ancient times, the Tung were a matrilineal people, and women led the tribe, not men. Sa-sui, or Pi-pen as she was called before her deification, led the Tung in resisting the encroachment of the Han Chinese. But there were simply too many of them, and eventually she found herself surrounded by her enemies. Instead of accepting defeat, she jumped off a cliff together with her two daughters, who normally would have succeeded her. But instead of disappearing from the scene, Pi-pen's spirit continued to lead the Tung in resisting the confiscation of their land. But it was no use, and eventually she led her people further south to a new homeland, where they have lived ever since.

According to my self-appointed guide, whenever the Tung build a new village, the first structure they put up is a shrine to Pi-pen, or Sa-sui. And whenever the Tung meet with adversity, they think Sa-sui has abandoned them, and they sacrifice at her shrine to call her back. And at the beginning of the year, they sing and dance for three days and nights and ask Sa-sui to protect them for another year.

Like the other ethnic minorities who live in this part of China, the Tung support themselves by growing rice. But they also raise fish. Every village is surrounded by dozens of fishponds full of carp and crayfish—

The village of Chengyang

and Chengyang was no exception. After visiting the village's drum tower and shrine, I followed the young man who had become my de facto guide. He led me down another dirt trail to another Tung village and invited me to his home for lunch. It took about two hours to prepare, and it included the usual plates of pork and the vegetable of the month. The man's wife also brought out, as a special treat, a kind of dried fish that the Tung served at important occasions. I felt honored and took a bite. But even the smallest bite was too much. Even now, I can't quite remember if it was incredibly salty, incredibly sour, or just incredibly rotten. Maybe it was all three. In any case, if you visit a Tung village and someone asks you to try the dried fish, you're on your own.

Once I got past the special treat, I thanked my hosts and told them I had to return to Sanchiang. After recrossing the bridge, I waited on the road for a bus back to town. While I was waiting, a number of logging trucks rumbled past. In addition to augmenting their diet with fish, the Tung supplement their income with lumber. In fact, the mountains around Sanchiang are among China's major lumber-producing areas, thanks largely to the efforts of the Tung. The Tung love trees, which isn't

Stone-lined hearth

surprising, considering their kinship. Their favorite is the fir. Whenever
a child is born, the parents plant a stand of fir saplings. The Tung say it
takes about eighteen years for a stand of fir trees to mature, just in time
to become a new house for a new married couple. Just think what the
world would look like if we all did that. Nowadays, all we have is Arbor
Day to remind us of our lost connection to trees. And after we plant a
small sapling that probably won't last through the summer, back we go
to our cement-surrounded lives. Eventually, the bus came, and I waved
goodbye to the tree stump people.

鎮遠

7. Chenyuan

ONCE I MADE IT back to Sanchiang, the most natural route would have been to continue west into the province of Kueichou. Unfortunately, a range of mountains made travel between Kuanghsi and Kueichou just about impossible. The few dirt roads that traversed the mountains were closed to foreigners without special permits and guides. After collecting my gear and checking out of the hotel, I had no choice but to take the afternoon train. The train station was a thirty-minute bus ride away, and there were only two trains a day: one going north, and one going south. I bought a ticket on the two o'clock heading north to Huaihua. It was the local, and it was painfully slow. But at least there were plenty of seats.

About the only thing I worry about when traveling in China is whether I can stay in a town long enough to wash my clothes. Of course, the washing isn't the hard part. It's the drying. What usually happens is that I end up carrying around damp clothes for a few days until I stay somewhere long enough or arrive early enough. I didn't arrive in Huaihua until eight o'clock that night, and I skipped the clothes washing altogether and went straight to bed. I didn't even bother with dinner.

Early the next morning, I walked back across the street to the train station and took the first train heading southwest toward Chenyuan. The train was the seven-twenty-five local, and I remember it well because halfway to Chenyuan, a lady the size of a gorilla got on and sat down beside me. As soon as she sat down, she burst into tears. Her husband, she said, had run off with another woman and all her money too, and she was going to Chenyuan to kill him. Between sobs, she blamed her troubles on the country's leaders. Everyone knew, she said, that Teng Hsiao-p'ing used the people's money to support his relatives and his girl-friends. As soon as she said this, all the passengers in the car covered up their ears in unison. I was amazed at the reaction. It was such an imme-diate and unequivocal gesture, it seemed planned. But it wasn't. This was what people did in China in those days when they heard someone criticizing the country's leaders. And so we continued on to Chenyuan looking like a trainload of fools, hearing no evil. It was so funny, I had a hard time keeping from laughing while also trying to sympathize with the woman's plight.

I tried to look out the window. But there wasn't anything to see. All I could see were clouds. They were so low, even the treetops weren't visible. That was how I entered Kueichou, which had to be the most sun-forsaken province in China. And my first stop in that sun-forsaken land was the town of Chenyuan, which straddled the Wuyang, or Sun-less, River. How fitting, I thought, as the train pulled up to the platform. Sun or no sun, I hurried out of the car to avoid having to deal with the jilted wife bent on revenge. As I disembarked, instead of the usual flock of taxi drivers, I was met by a gaggle of farmers, one of whom led me to his pony cart. It was even outfitted with an awning. It turned out the train station was two kilometers from the center of town, and the pony cart drivers had a monopoly on transportation. At a cost of 1RMB, or 20 cents, it was the perfect introduction to what was about to become one of my favorite towns.

While we clip-clopped our way down the cobblestone road into Chenyuan, I asked my driver about the merits of the town's hotels. He suggested the brand-new Wuyang Guesthouse about halfway into town, and that was where I got off. It turned out to be a good choice. The staff was friendly, the room was clean, and the price was right: 5RMB, or 1 buck. I pushed back the window curtain and discovered that my room also had a view of the Wuyang River. The clouds had lifted and revealed a town hemmed in by mountains. It was such a fine view, it took a while before I realized there were pigs grunting below my room. Even though it was a two-storey hotel, it was built like a traditional Chuang or Yao house, except that my room came with its own latrine. A few minutes later, the concierge brought me two thermoses of hot water, and I asked her if there were any boats that took passengers along the river. She said I was in luck. There was a tour leaving in ten minutes.

As it turned out, the Wuyang Guesthouse was only two hundred meters from the office of China Travel, which had been granted sole authority to organize tours along the river that flowed through Chenyuan. During the tourist season, from April through September, there was a morning tour and an afternoon tour. Although I had arrived in March, a group of Chinese tourists had arranged a private tour, and I was just in time to join them for a modest 18RMB, or less than 4 dollars.

The tour began with a thirty-minute bus ride across the plateau northwest of town to a section of the Wuyang River that ten years earlier had been declared a protected scenic area. After a short walk, we boarded a flat-bottomed boat with hard benches and an awning to protect passengers from the rain. But there was no protection from the wind. During the previous twenty-four hours, the temperature had dropped from twenty degrees Celsius to five, and the wind was blowing away those last five. It was freezing. Obviously, the time to take the Wuyang River cruise was not March. I was wearing my silk underwear, but it wasn't helping. I was truly cold. We looked like a boatload of hunchbacks, as we all cowered down as low as we could. Two hundred years earlier, the local authorities had decided to disguise the original name of the river by adding a water radical to one of the Chinese characters that made up its name so that people would think they were traveling on the Sunny Wu River. But this was the Sunless River, and even a fire radical wouldn't have made any difference. We all sat shivering on our benches as we began our three-hour pleasure cruise.

As we pushed off, we lifted our heads above the boat's sides just enough to see a natural stone bridge high up in the cliffs. Then the wind forced us back down. For the next hour, we cruised downstream oblivious to everything but our frozen extremities. According to our guide,

Peacock Rock on the Wuyang River

we passed through a gorge that was about a hundred meters wide and a couple hundred meters high and lined with waterfalls and caves and the usual assortment of strangely shaped rocks. After about five kilometers, the downstream portion of the cruise ended just below a huge stone pinnacle shaped like a peacock. We all looked up, then resumed the fetal position as we turned and headed back upstream. Our agony, though, was somewhat relieved by an unscheduled stop in a secluded bay to enforce the laws that ten years earlier had made this a protected area, which included the trees.

The crew spotted a dugout pulled up along the bank and went to investigate. In the bushes they discovered two impoverished-looking men and a stack of several hundred freshly cut saplings. The two men pulled out their sickles to let the crew know they were not to be trifled with. But our skipper was a sly dog. He grabbed a rope that was tied to their dugout, and a few seconds later their boat belonged to the state, as did their rear ends. There was no way out of the gorge without a boat. At last we had something to talk about besides the cold.

Finally, we returned to Chenyuan, where I restored feeling to my extremities by holding my hands and feet against the radiator in my room. When they were finally usable again, I walked outside then down the road to the only restaurant I could see. At least it was warm inside. Afterwards, I returned to my room and spent the night under my blankets, with all my clothes on.

The next morning, I was still alive, and I was still in Chenyuan. A few days before the end of 1986, the Chinese government added thirty-six cities to its initial list of thirty historically important urban centers, making them eligible for state funds to restore cultural sites. Among the additional thirty-six were Shanghai, Tienchin, Shenyang, Wuhan, Nanchang, Chungching, and Chenyuan. Chenyuan? Where in blazes was Chenyuan? everyone must have asked. And what was it doing on the list?

The reason Chenyuan was terra incognita was that this area encompassed by the provinces of Kueichou and Yunnan wasn't part of the Middle Kingdom until seven hundred years ago. And it wasn't the Chinese but the Mongols who wrested control from the tribal chieftains who had ruled this area up until then. Less than a hundred years later, the Mongols were back in the Central Asian steppes herding horses and sheep, and the Chinese were back in control of China, including the newly conquered Southwest territories.

A Chinese general sent to survey the situation wrote back to his superiors: "Whoever holds Chenyuan holds the key to the Southwest." And so Chenyuan became the key. Due to China's topography, the only way an army could enter the area was via Kuangchou to the southeast or via Chengtu to the northwest. But both routes involved crossing impenetrable mountains. Meanwhile, a boat on the Yangtze could turn south into Tungting Lake, then sail southwest up the Yuan River and finally into the Wuyang River and travel all the way to Chenyuan. That was why Chenyuan was included among China's most historically important cities.

As soon as China gained control of the Kueichou-Yunnan region seven hundred years ago, Chenyuan became the conduit through which the central authorities shipped in armies and merchants shipped out raw materials. This, though, was as far as their boats went. Beyond Chenyuan, the Wuyang River was too shallow for anything but small dugouts, so this was where goods were off-loaded.

Traces of Chenyuan's commercial importance weren't hard to find. Steps that once led to the loading platforms could still be seen at the former quays along the river. While I was deciding how to spend my day in Chenyuan, the concierge told me that for a couple RMB I could hire a boatman to pole me along the embankment for a closer look. But the wind hadn't relented. It was still freezing. She also suggested the Sea Goddess Shrine at the base of the cliffs at the west edge of town. The shrine, she said, was built by merchants from Fuchien, who also built their own guildhall in Chenyuan, as did the merchants of seven other provinces. The guildhalls sounded far more interesting, if only because the oldest, biggest, and best preserved of them was just down the road at the east edge of town. After a breakfast of hot soybean milk and steamed buns at the hotel restaurant, I boarded another one of the pony carts that made a visit to Chenyuan such an unexpected pleasure. There were a few cars in town, but I didn't see a taxi the whole time I was there.

Even at pony-cart speed, we arrived at the Chianghsi Guildhall in a matter of minutes. The guildhall's courtyards and galleries were being restored, and its main building had been converted into a museum devoted to the houses and other wooden structures built by the province's ethnic minorities. On one of the museum walls there was a map showing the location of all the wooden structures of historical significance in Kueichou. In addition to the map, there were detailed architectural drawings. But even more impressive were the models. There were large-scale models of a Tung covered bridge, a Tung drum tower, and typical houses of the Tung, the Miao, and the Puyi minorities. For anyone with an interest in the details of architecture or construction common to these tribes, this was a truly amazing place. I saw similar exhibits in the provincial museums of Southwest China, but none came close to the detail in construction and the care in presentation.

View of Chenyuan and Chusheng Bridge from Blue Dragon Cave

After lingering over the house models, I passed through a courtyard and entered a second hall that contained examples of carving and wood-work used in house interiors. A group of carpenters were also using the hall as a workspace. They didn't have any machine tools, only the tra-ditional hand tools used elsewhere in the world: plumb lines, handsaws, and planes. In addition to the guildhall, they were also restoring the various shrines and pavilions that made up the Blue Dragon Cave com-plex in the cliffs above the guildhall, which was where I headed next.

More than two thousand years ago, China's Taoists developed a sys-tem of symbols that assigned the color black and the turtle-snake to the north, the color white and the tiger to the west, the color red and the phoenix to the south, and the color blue and the dragon to the east. Since Chenyuan was situated at the eastern edge of China's newly con-quered southwest territories, a blue dragon was chosen as the symbol for the city five hundred years ago, and it has remained its symbol ever since.

The cave complex actually included three caves, of which Blue Dragon, or Chinglungtung, was but one. The shrines were intended not as residences for monks or priests, but rather as places where the city's military and merchant elite could supplicate spirits, be they Buddhist, Taoist, or non-aligned, to ensure the success of their undertakings. The caves themselves weren't much to look at. Blue Dragon was filled with mud and rocks and was no longer accessible, and the other two were merely overhangs. Also, the statues that once graced their niches and altars were long gone. Still, to walk through the intricate system of stairways, pavilions, and galleries that extended across the cliff was to walk back five hundred years. All I had to do to go back to the Ming dynasty was look through the lattice windows and past the tiled roofs below and across the dark waters of the Wuyang River. Squeezed between the river and the cliff on the opposite shore were hundreds of ancient houses and no sign of the twentieth century. Chenyuan's residential quarter, it turned out, was its most famous museum.

When I visited in early March, carpenters were just beginning work on the final addition to this wonderful view: a tea pavilion opposite the guildhall entrance overlooking the Wuyang River. No doubt it was going to be a fine place to sip a cup of tea, or wine. But it wasn't ready. Besides, the weather was still freezing. Since I had no choice but to keep moving, I decided to cross the ancient stone bridge that led from the guildhall to the old residential part of town on the north side of the river.

It was called the Chusheng Bridge, first built in 1372 and last rebuilt in 1723. It was wide enough and strong enough for vehicle traffic. In fact, during the Ch'ing dynasty, Burma's ambassador to China rode across this bridge on his elephant. But neither elephants nor cars were allowed anymore. The bridge was considered too important to risk damaging and was limited to pedestrians. And to make sure, there was now a pavilion in the middle.

Once across, I walked down the road that led into the center of town. But before I got that far, I turned off to investigate some of the alleys. Students of architecture came from all over China to study the houses. Just before I reached the town's other bridge, one built for vehicle traffic, I turned off one last time and followed a set of steps that zigzagged up the side of the cliff that hemmed in the houses. The path led to Ssukungtien, a shrine built in the Ch'ing dynasty to honor four generals who had led the Chinese fight against the tribes in that area 2,500 years ago. I paused at the shrine long enough to catch my breath. The reason I was making the effort was that the path supposedly led to the wall that kept the hill tribes out of the rest of China.

The construction of the wall marked Chenyuan's beginning as a garrison town, and it remained a garrison town until its importance as an entrepôt for trade began to overshadow its strategic importance. That was back in the Ming dynasty, when the Chinese recovered the throne from the Mongols. Despite claiming the new Southwest territories conquered by the Mongols, the Chinese were never really able to enforce their authority beyond Chenyuan, and Chenyuan remained the limit of Chinese influence. To make sure the tribes of Kueichou stayed on their side of the mountains, the Chinese built a wall on either side of Chenyuan, forcing anyone entering or leaving the area to do so via the Wuyang River.

While I was catching my breath at the shrine to the four generals, some school children walked by on their way home. I asked if they knew where the old wall was. They did, and I followed them to the top of the cliff. They pointed past a series of terraced fields, and a few minutes later, I was walking on top of the wall. Its stone facing and brick interior were crumbling, but it was in good enough condition for me to follow its perambulations until it ended abruptly at the edge of the cliff. Far below flowed the dark serpent of the Wuyang River. Not far downstream, the wall began again on the other side and undulated into the distance. As far as I could see, the wall was barbarian-proof, except, of course, for me.

Standing on top of that wall, I shivered in the freezing wind that hadn't stopped since I had arrived. It was time to move on. One place I had heard about that I would have visited if I had had more time was the Miao village of Paoching, thirty-five kilometers to the south. The guide on the Wuyang River cruise said it was one of the more primitive Miao villages in that part of China. But he said I needed a permit, and I didn't feel up to the red tape.

As I made my way down from the wall, I passed the temple that honored the four generals again. I stopped long enough to use my binoculars to look across the adjacent ravine into a cave that was partially blocked by sheets of tattered red cloth. In ancient times it had been the residence of a Taoist monk whose name nobody remembered, and now it was home to a ragamuffin man and his ragamuffin wife and their ragamuffin children. I wondered if the man was a Taoist or just poor. But it was too cold to find out. I continued down the trail to the one road that ran through town and followed a couple of pigs to the bus station, where I bought a ticket to Shihping, forty-six kilometers to the west. The bus wasn't due to leave for an hour, which gave me just enough time to return to my hotel and collect my gear. I was so quick that I got back to the station with thirty minutes to spare. It was the cold that made me move so fast. As I walked back into the building, I couldn't help but notice that the temperature inside the station was lower than the temperature outside. While I was deciding whether to walk back outside, the stationmaster took pity on me and invited me into the dispatch room, where the drivers were sitting around a charcoal stove. I joined them, and for the first time in two days I felt my toes.

苗族

8. The Miao

ABOUT THE TIME my fingers and toes stopped throbbing, the stationmaster said it was time for my bus. And so I headed for Shihping. Shihping wasn't on the train line. The only way to get there on public transportation was by bus. The reason I wanted to go there was that Shihping was in the middle of Miao country. The Miao were among the oldest-known ethnic groups in China. They were mentioned on oracle bones dating back to the Shang dynasty, nearly four thousand years ago. But the history of the Miao went back even earlier to the time of the Yellow Emperor, or 2600 BC. The Yellow Emperor, or Huang-ti, was the leader of a confederation of tribes in North China along the Yellow River. The Yellow Emperor's ascendancy and that of the ancestors of the Han Chinese began when he defeated a rival group of tribes led by Ch'ih You.

During my journey up the Yellow River in 1991, I passed the salt lake in southern Shansi where the final battle took place. Following Ch'ih You's defeat, the tribes that had aligned themselves with him were forced to leave the Yellow River watershed and migrate south. Among those tribes were the ancestors of the Miao, and the Miao still traced their ancestry to Ch'ih You. My own migration was simpler. An hour and a half after leaving Chenyuan, I was walking down one of Shihping's two paved streets along with Ch'ih You's descendants and wondering what China's history would have been like if Ch'ih You had gained control of that salt lake. Salt was crucial to preserving enough food to form urban centers and to fight wars. Without a limitless supply of salt, the ancestors of the Miao were unable to form or maintain the kind of civilization that developed along the Yellow River. And so they headed south, and the valleys and mountains around Shihping were home to thousands of their descendents.

Shihping, like Chenyuan, straddled the sunless Wuyang River. But Shihping was about one-tenth the size, and the majority of its residents weren't Han Chinese but Miao. The Miao were China's fourth-largest ethnic minority, after the Chuang, the Manchus, and the Hui. In 1990, the government census counted 7.5 million Miao in China scattered throughout the Southwest, with the greatest concentration in Kueichou.

For my part, I was glad to find myself among Ch'ih You's descendents. Although Ch'ih You was the earliest semihistorical ancestor of the Miao, and no Miao festival is complete without a nod in his direction, the original ancestor of the Miao wasn't a person at all, but a tree stump. Does that sound familiar? Like the Tung, the Miao also trace their ancestry back to a stump—but not just any stump, a maple stump. This paricular maple stump gave birth to a butterfly, and the butterfly laid twelve eggs in the foam that lined the stump's bark. And from the twelve eggs came Dragon, Tiger, Snake, Centipede, good spirits and evil spirits, and Chiang-yang, the earliest human. When Chiang-yang's butterfly mother died, her spirit floated up to the sky and became the moon, and to this day the Miao word for "moon" still means "mother."

And so there I was once more among the tree-stump people. Being one-tenth the size of Chenyuan, Shihping didn't offer much in the way of lodging. Everyone I asked at the bus station pointed me to the Shihping County Government Hostel, which was only two blocks away. It was clean, and there was a radiator in my room. But it was too early to call it a day, and after dropping my bag in my room, I walked back to the town's main street. Actually, calling Shihping a town might be going a bit too far. Still, it was bigger than a village, and Shihping boasted two paved streets that intersected at a market, to which I then proceeded. While I was walking among the produce stalls, I was approached by two Miao girls who wanted to practice their English. They said they had graduated from high school and were waiting for the right job to come along. That sounded familiar. I told them to be patient. I had to wait thirty years for the right job, namely getting paid to travel around China and write the two-minute pieces of radio fluff that made up the original version of this book.

While I continued walking through the market, and they continued asking me the standard set of get-acquainted questions, I asked them if there were any traditional Miao products for sale in town. I didn't see anything in the market, and it seemed like there should be handicrafts of some sort for sale. After all, Shihping was surrounded by dozens of Miao villages. The girls discussed the matter in Miao, then led me back to the town's one and only intersection. A few doors down East Street, they led me through a doorway. A small sign said I had just entered the Shihping County National Minority Embroidery Factory.

Inside the doorway, they led me up a set of stairs to the second floor and introduced me to Comrade Liu. Comrade Liu said she had started the factory with her own money a few years earlier, and it was now the biggest employer in town. Inside the main workroom, forty Miao women were embroidering quilt covers and pillowcases and shawls. She then led me into a small showroom, where I proceeded to exchange all the cash in my pockets for the most incredible piece of embroidery I had ever laid eyes or hands on.

I had already bought an embroidered jacket in the Yao village of Ailing and thought it was the most incredible piece of sewing I had ever seen. But my Yao jacket now had competition in the form of a silk shawl embroidered on both sides with the identical pattern. I don't know how the Miao women did it, but I don't part with 100 bucks easily, which was what I paid for a huge black silk shawl covered on both sides with hundreds of flowers and vines and, of course, butterflies, one of the ancestors of the Miao people. But what was so impressive about the embroidery was that it didn't follow traditional forms, the butterflies notwithstanding. It was the artistic creation of a Miao woman who worked at the factory. I saw a similar shawl later at a shop in Hong

Miao woman offering the de rigueur oxhorn of rice wine

Kong selling for five times what it cost in Shihping, and it still looked like a bargain. There was sewing, and then there was Miao embroidery. I finally tore myself free and said goodbye to the factory's owner and the two Miao girls who had led me there, then continued down the main street to the traffic circle at the east edge of town.

On the north side of the circle was the road that brought me into town, and on the south side was the local office of China Travel. I walked inside. Normally, I avoided China Travel, preferring to spend my money on embroidered shawls. But I felt lucky, and I have to admit, if every office of China Travel was as good as the one in Shihping, I would make theirs my first stop in every town. For a modest 30RMB, or 6 dollars, they arranged to take me to a Miao wedding banquet. In a matter of minutes I was walking across the bridge that spanned the Wuyang River to a nearby village where there was a wedding in progress.

The actual ceremony was still a few days away, but the celebration had begun ten days earlier with visits by a constant stream of relatives and guests congratulating the families of the bride and groom. My guide led me to the house of the groom, where I stopped at the doorway to drink a horn of wine. During such celebrations, the Miao hang two buffalo horns inside their doorway. Whenever a guest arrives, both horns are filled with rice wine, and the guest drains one while the host or another family member drains the other.

I drained mine and stepped inside, but not before pausing to let the groom's mother mark my cheeks and forehead with the base of a dried thistle flower that she had first dipped in green dye. Within seconds my face was covered with green sunbursts, as if I had contracted some new kind of measles. She said it would let everyone know I had been a guest at a Miao celebration, and unless I used soap to wash it off, the dye would stay on my face for a week. Even under normal conditions, I attracted crowds. Now people were going to think the circus was in town—or a plague.

When I finally stepped inside, I saw several men whose faces were also covered with green sunbursts sitting on benches around the fire that dominated the middle of the house. Outside, it was freezing. In fact, the sky looked like it would be snowing before the day was done. But a Miao wedding celebration was guaranteed to drive away the cold, especially once you learned how to say, "Pass the buffalo horn, please."

As I sat down on one of the benches that surrounded the fire pit, my guide told me that the bride was sitting in the next room. She had arrived ten days earlier. According to Miao custom, the wedding would take place after she had been there for thirteen days. The celebration would then last for three more days, and immediately afterwards she would return to her own village and stay there for the next two years. She wouldn't move into her husband's house until their first child was a year old.

Apparently, that gave the husband's family time to build a new house for the couple and forced the husband to be on good terms with his in-laws—since that was the only way he was going to see his wife. It also gave the wife a chance to have her first child in more familiar surroundings. This wasn't just a Miao practice: most of the tribes I visited on my trip told me they followed the same tradition.

While I was sitting there, the women in the groom's family were preparing a huge meal, and a buffalo horn full of rice wine was making the rounds. Between horns, I looked around. I couldn't help noticing a pair of new coffins stored above me in the rafters. The Han Chinese consider even the sight of a coffin inauspicious, and one of the greatest insults is to have one delivered to someone's house while they are still alive. But my Miao host beamed with pride and explained that the coffins were for him and his wife. He said the Miao believe that old people aren't truly happy unless they get their coffin ready before they die.

Meanwhile, my host announced that the meal was ready. His wife pulled a foot-long hairpin out of her hair and stirred the coals, then put it back in her hair, and the meal began. Moving around the fire, she used her chopsticks to put a bite of food into everyone's mouth. Then her husband poured everyone a bowl of white lightning.

Usually the Miao preferred rice wine, but it was freezing outside, and something stronger was called for. But before anyone drank, they all dipped the ends of their chopsticks into their cups and flicked a few drops of liquor onto the ground. They did this three times. My host explained that this was to honor the ancestral spirits. The Miao loved to drink even after they were dead. My host added that a person's true spirit only appeared when he was drunk, to which everyone nodded in agreement.

After a few rounds of white lightning, we moved on to the food. By this time, everything was a blur, but I remember the pork fat, which I dipped into a sauce flavored with vinegar and red peppers. My host told me that vinegar and red peppers were the favorite spices of the Miao. And that was all I remember.

It was probably a good thing I visited a few days before the wedding. Once the wedding begins, no one is allowed to lie down for three days. If you have to sleep, or if you get too drunk to hold up your head, you can lean against the wall, or you can be tied there. When I visited there was already one guest with a rope under his arms holding him against the wall. The Miao hate party-poopers. Like the Yao, Miao hosts hate to see a guest leave sober, and in my case, I didn't offend their custom.

After thanking the man and his wife for their hospitality, I went back outside into the cold and floated across the bridge that spanned the Wuyang River. I asked the man from China Travel who had escorted me to the wedding about the possibility of a river cruise. Apparently the alcohol had blurred my memory of my previous trip along the same river near Chenyuan. He told me that the section upstream from Shihping was much wilder and had only been opened to tourism the previous year. He said there were lots of wild animals in the upstream section, including wild oxen and monkeys. In the old days, he said, small boats went upstream as far as the town of Huangping, and the monkeys threw rocks at anyone who didn't stop to leave some food along the shore. But there was no regular boat service. China Travel, he said, offered a four-hour cruise to those who showed up with enough money. But as the alcohol began to wear off, and I began to wince at the freezing wind again, I dropped the subject and concentrated on trying to walk straight. Maybe next time, I thought. Next time I would come in summer instead of spring.

In ancient times, the Chinese divided spring into nine nine-day periods, and I was barely into the fifth period. During the first two periods everything is still frozen, then during the next two periods streams begin to flow, and during the fifth and sixth periods trees begin to bud. I had clearly not arrived at the seventh or eighth period when people begin to wear fewer clothes. I had everything on, including my silk long johns and my parka, and I was still cold. Nor was I anywhere near the ninth and final period of spring when the weather warms up enough to sit on a rock.

Just in case I needed a reminder of that, while I was staggering toward my hotel, it began to snow. Once I made it back, I buried myself beneath all the blankets in my room and considered my next destination. If the weather had been warmer, I might have taken a bus southwest to Huangping. Halfway to Huangping was Feiyuntung, the oldest Buddhist temple in the province. And just north of Huangping was the airstrip the Flying Tigers used for refueling during World War II. But the next big town to the west of Shihping was Kaili, and I had heard that there was a hotel in Kaili that had bathtubs and hot water.

The prospect of a hot bath won out. The next morning I took one of the buses that left Shihping every hour. Twenty kilometers later, it dropped me and most of the other passengers off at a train station in the middle of nowhere where one train stopped every afternoon. The train was an hour late, and it was freezing. Once again I was rescued by the stationmaster, who invited me into the ticket office, where I joined a group of elderly Miao women sitting around a potbellied stove. The stationmaster said the women were from the village of Shuangching, another twenty kilometers to the southeast. She said it was one of the most remote Miao settlements in the county, and the women had come down to attend a wedding at another village further down the line. They asked me to join them. My face was still covered with the traces of green dye. But one wedding was enough. All I wanted was a hot bath.

Eventually the train came, and we all climbed aboard and even found seats. A few minutes later, the conductor came through to check tickets and asked me to follow him into the next car. He unlocked the door and relocked it behind me. It was the first time I had been in an empty train car in China. I didn't think there was such a thing. Then he asked me if I wanted to exchange some money. It turned out I was in the money exchange car. I didn't have any dollars, which was what he wanted. He said, "If I could just get some dollars, I could really do something." I wasn't sure what it was he could do with dollars, but out of politeness I exchanged a few hundred FEC (foreign exchange certificates—the only Chinese currency foreigners could legally get in those days). Then he left, and I had the car to myself.

A couple stops later, the conductor returned with another man. The other man was holding a rather large screwdriver, and he proceeded to wave it in front of my face, while the conductor noted that it would not be a good idea to tell anyone about our little exchange. I couldn't believe it. I was actually being threatened by this jerk of a conductor and his thug friend. I forced myself to laugh, since the only alternative was to cry. I resolved to follow the path of upright living in the future and never let myself be led into an empty train car again.

It was with great relief that I disembarked in the town of Kaili. My relief, though, was short lived. Kaili turned out to be an industrial armpit of a town. There were smokestacks everywhere. And the snow had turned to slush. After dropping my gear at the Kaili Guesthouse, I slogged my way through the mud to visit what was allegedly the only ethnic minority museum in the province. It was in a huge new building on a hill at the edge of town. But it was locked, and the man with the key was gone. Back at my hotel I learned that even if he had been there, he wouldn't have let me in. Foreigners who wanted to visit the museum had to apply at the local office of foreign affairs or at China Travel— incredible, but true.

Since the office of China Travel was just inside the hotel's front gate, I walked over and asked about visiting the museum. After a phone call, they said the man with the key was gone for the day, so that was out. They then handed me a brochure for the Miao village of Langte, and it was in English: "Hidden at the foot of Leikung Mountain is the little mountain village of Langte consisting of several dozens of households.

Green trees and bamboo groves make the little village a picturesque scenery. Waterwheels on the Wangfeng River in front of the village sing the ancient Miao songs day and night. While rows of wooden houses sit listening on the slope of the mountain. The houses are all supported on wooden poles and lined with curvy wooden banisters on the upper floors. A genuine Miao style indeed. And all the paths in the village are paved with flagstones, neat and tidy as a park. This is one of the first batch of open-air ethnic museums in Kueichou." The brochure even had some pictures of guests drinking rice wine out of buffalo horns, which looked pretty good. But as with Kaili's ethnic minority museum, all non-Chinese visitors had to have a permit, which meant they had to join a tour or hire their own guide. I passed up the picturesque little village of Langte and returned to the hotel for my long-awaited bath. I even washed my clothes and dried them over the radiator.

The next morning I decided that since I needed a permit to do anything in or around Kaili, it was time to move on. The only good things I remember about Kaili were that I finally got my hot bath and that there were trains leaving almost every hour. By early afternoon, I was in Kueiyang. Since this was the provincial capital of Kueichou, I decided to splurge and checked into the Plaza Hotel. And at a supermarket right across the street, I bought what was probably the last bottle of Canadian Club in town for the same amount I paid for my room, 96RMB, or 20 bucks. Yes indeed, a bottle of CC and a heated room with a carpet and a bathtub and a phone that connected me with the whole world, all for 40 bucks, was a pretty good deal in China, and I called home for the first time since I had started traveling south of the clouds. Everyone still remembered me, and while I sipped my whiskey, I bragged about losing a few pounds since beginning my reduced-beer diet. Two days earlier, I had actually had to take my belt in a notch to keep my pants on.

貴陽

9. Kueiyang

THE NEXT DAY I was off to see the sights. Right across the street from my hotel I caught a bus to the provincial museum at the north edge of town. I always tried to begin my tour of a city with the local museum, if for no other reason than that every museum had a museum store, and every museum store sold maps and books about the area. But Kueichou was one of China's poorest provinces, and all I found in the provincial museum store was one dusty copy of a tourist brochure.

I moved on to the exhibits, which included the standard displays of minority paraphernalia and a wing featuring a stuffed python sneaking up on a stuffed magpie and a tree full of stuffed monkeys picking stuffed fleas off each other. There was also a fairly good collection of stuffed birds and animals, but that was about all. So much for the museum. I moved on.

My next destination was Chinlingshan, a mountain at the north edge of town just two bus stops past the museum. Chin is the old name for Kueichou, and "lingshan" means "magic mountain." Over the previous few decades, though, Chinlingshan had lost whatever magic it once possessed. It was now Kueiyang's main recreation center, complete with the standard lake full of paddle-wheelers, your basic dust-covered zoo, and trails lined with more vendors than trees. Just inside the main gate, I passed a funhouse. A mechanical Judge of Hell was sitting outside the entrance checking names in his register. Since he obviously hadn't gotten around to mine, I passed him and his funhouse by.

I continued past a dozen old men airing their songbirds in the park's leafless trees and two old ladies washing their laundry in a lotusless pond. The main trail continued on to Chilintung, or Unicorn Cave. During World War II, Chiang Kai-shek used the cave as a prison for Chang Hsueh-liang and Yang Hu-ch'eng, the two Nationalist generals who arrested him in Sian and forced him to begin fighting the invading Japanese instead of the Communists. I admired the two generals for that, but I passed their former prison by. Too many of the caves I had visited smelled like urinals. Just past the cave, I left the main trail and headed instead for Chinlingshan itself. Chinlingshan wasn't a big mountain, but it was a famous mountain, and I imagine even the monkeys I passed along the trail knew the story about the monk responsible for its fame.

A long time ago, the governor of Kueiyang had a daughter who fell ill. Her body swelled up like that of a blowfish, and none of the city's doctors were able to cure her, which wasn't surprising considering that they had been forced to come to the palace and were paid nothing for their trouble. It turned out that the governor was very rich and was the city's biggest landowner, but he was also the city's biggest miser. As his daughter's condition worsened, and as the governor became increasingly worried, in desperation he announced he would give a reward of two thousand ounces of gold to anyone who could cure her. But to make sure that every quack in town didn't try to claim the money at his daughter's expense, he added that anyone who tried and failed would receive two thousand blows.

For ten days no one came forward. Finally, on the eleventh day an old monk named Ch'ih-sung, or Red Pine, appeared, and he wrote down a prescription. When the governor had the prescription filled, sure enough his daughter recovered. But when the monk came to claim his reward, the governor just laughed. He said his daughter's recovery was the will of Heaven and had nothing to do with the monk's medicine. The wicked governor then ordered the monk to be given two thousand blows. A hundred blows, let alone two thousand, would have been enough to kill most people, but Red Pine was no ordinary monk. He possessed magic powers. He just laughed the whole time he was being beaten, and when he finally left, he told the governor that the next time they met, the governor would be on the receiving end. The governor was speechless, but before he could have the monk beaten again, Red Pine vanished.

The next day, wouldn't you know, the governor's daughter suddenly fell into a coma, and the governor had no choice but to ask Red Pine to come back. He even gave the monk the gold he owed him. Red Pine said the governor still owed him two thousand blows, but since he was a monk he would take a piece of land instead. All he wanted was a piece the size of his robe. Naturally, the miserly governor agreed. The monk then threw his robe into the air, and it became as big as a cloud and covered the whole mountain where he lived, which was Chinlingshan, the mountain I was now walking up. The monk then cured the governor's daughter and gave the gold to the city's poor, and he built a temple further up the trail at the end of its twenty-four zigs and twenty-four zags.

It was called Hungfu Temple, and it was still there when I arrived. But it was undergoing renovation, and the place was a mess. Despite the temple's strange beginning and its beautiful setting, just below the summit of Chinlingshan, it wasn't that interesting. Just another place to light incense and donate money. I lit and donated my share and walked through the stupa cemetery behind the temple, wondering if Red Pine's magic powers did him any good in the Great Beyond. While I was wondering, it began snowing again, and I headed back down the mountain, pausing to warm my hands around a cup of hot tea sold by a trailside vendor and snacking on some fry-bread sold by another. Then I boarded a bus that took me across town to Kueiyang's southern suburbs.

As I passed through the city, my nostrils winced at the acrid coal smoke without which no Chinese city was complete in winter. I covered my mouth and nostrils with my hand and kept it there until the bus dropped me off at Kueiyang's most famous sight: Chiahsiulou, a pavilion built in the middle of the Nanming River. "Chia-hsiu" means "armored flower," referring to two iron pillars erected in front of the pavilion that looked like a flower's stamens. The iron came from the captured weapons of the minority groups that were crazy enough to rebel against Chinese rule.

The pavilion was a striking piece of architecture in an equally striking setting. It was built in 1597 on a huge rock in the middle of the river to commemorate the completion of a dike to control flooding. It had been rebuilt several times and was connected to both sides of the river by a bridge. I walked out to the middle of the river and looked inside the three-storey structure. It was empty, except for an exhibition of the kind of furniture designed to get rid of guests as soon as possible. I took the hint. As I came out of the pavilion, I noticed an even more impressive piece of architecture going up on the other side of the river. It was Kuanyin Temple, rising from the ashes of the Cultural Revolution. Since the temple was far from finished, I headed back toward my hotel.

A few blocks short of the Plaza, I stopped again on a side street to inspect another ancient pavilion. It was called the Wenchangko and was built in 1609, a few years after the Chiahsiulou. But unlike the Chiahsiulou, which looked awfully lonesome in the middle of the river, the Wenchangko was connected to other buildings and surrounded by a huge wall. It was, in fact, the city's center of learning back in the Ming and Ch'ing dynasties. During the 1940s the Kuomintang used it as a prison for misguided intellectuals. I couldn't help wondering at the irony. But it was boarded up, and my wonder subsided. I continued walking back to my hotel and began thinking about an early dinner and another hot bath and lying in bed with my bottle of Canadian Club. On the way, I passed a restaurant advertising p'i-chiu-ya, beer-fed duck, and looked at all the dead ducks hanging in the window. It made me appreciate my new reduced-beer diet.

Just past the duck gallows, I saw a sign for Yuan Chiao Vegetarian Restaurant. It was just off Yenan Road, one block west and three blocks south of the Plaza. I'm not sure how it began, but the restaurant had reopened several months earlier after a complete transformation into what looked like a traditional Chinese inn. It was actually a Buddhist temple, and the restaurant was run by the temple's nuns. I've lived in a few temples myself and eaten a lot of really good temple food, but the food at the Yuan Chiao was in a different class. It was as if some gourmet had tired of this mundane world and dedicated herself to preparing monastic cuisine for beings on a higher plane. I began with an hors d'oeuvre that included vegetarian sausage with walnuts and another consisting of sea moss with mushrooms, then I filled up on the standard luo-han-tsai, or monk's plate, which was far from standard. When I was done, I offered my congratulations to the chef, and, of course, to the Buddha.

It was a good thing I ate and bathed and slept so well in Kueiyang. The city was pretty much a bust otherwise. The museum's sole claim to fame was a bunch of stuffed birds, Chinlingshan's monks were upstaged by the mountain's monkeys, the city's famous Chiahsiulou Pavilion was now home to a Salvation Army furniture exhibit, and I had already bought the only bottle of whiskey in town. There was nothing left to do but to move on. About the only thing that might have kept me in Kueiyang was China's one and only liquor museum, established by the Kueichou Liquor Company, maker of China's most famous white lightning: Mao-t'ai. But when I learned that the factory and its museum were in Tsunyi, 150 kilometers to the north, I contented myself with my Canadian Club and resumed my westward journey the next morning.

安順

10. Anshun

THE NEXT BIG TOWN west of Kueiyang was Anshun, which was one-third the size with a mere half a million residents. Buses going there left from in front of the train station every thirty minutes or so, and I was on one of them by eight. I was there two hours later. The bus dropped me off at one end of the main street. The other end was the location of the town's train station. I followed the bus driver's recommendation and walked a few blocks east to the yellow-tiled facade of the Mintsu National Minority Hotel. I'm not sure what the hotel had to do with minorities, except it was on the austere side. The marble-tiled lobby was completely empty, except for a counter that stretched its entire width and a dozen haywire clocks on the wall above it that told visitors from Abu Dhabi to Zanzibar what time it was back home—a couple hours ago. The receptionists certainly weren't shy about asking for money. They wanted 100RMB, or 20 dollars, for a double, which was what I paid for a swank room at the Plaza in Kueiyang. Anshun was a provincial backwater, not the provincial capital, and fortunately the rate was negotiable. We ended up compromising at 50RMB.

I don't mean to disparage Anshun by calling it a backwater. Actually, I tend to enjoy backwaters more than I do provincial capitals, and within minutes of dropping my gear in my 10-dollar room, I was walking the backwater streets behind the hotel, browsing an endless series of market lanes. At one of them, I stopped to admire a man smoking tobacco rolled up and stuffed into the end of a long, curved bamboo pipe. He had used the pipe for so many years that the bamboo had turned red and the jade mouthpiece had turned yellow. He asked me if I wanted to buy it. I said, "Sure." He said 10RMB, and I said, "Sure." Then he rolled up a fresh leaf of tobacco and insisted I try it. I said, "Sure," and everything started to spin.

Once the spinning had slowed, I walked back out into the lane and continued wandering in the old part of town that stretched between the city's two major hotels, the Mintsu, where I was staying, and the Hungshan. The Hungshan was at the northeast edge of town. It was more modern and in a garden setting, and the rates were surprisingly lower. Also, there was an office of China Travel inside. But it was on the edge of town, a big drawback in a town that had only a few city buses, which was strange considering Anshun's size.

During my perambulations, I crossed a bridge and noticed a Buddhist Dharma wheel among the rooftops and went to investigate. It turned out to be a small temple, and inside I met an old monk who said he was living there while recuperating from an illness. He was the executive secretary of the province's Buddhist association and normally lived in Kueiyang. But the air in the capital, he said, wasn't fit to breathe, at least not in the winter, when everyone burned coal. I agreed with his choice and left him to his recuperation, and continued my aimless stroll through the old part of town.

A couple of zigs and zags later, I stopped at the city's Confucian temple, which was undergoing renovation. There were several very nice stone pillars carved with dragons, the woodwork of the renovated sections was excellent, and the workmen were friendly. But I continued on. A few blocks later, I stopped at a doorway covered by a white sheet. There was a red cross in the middle of the sheet, and a sign in English said MASSAGE. That was a word I loved to see, and I went inside. But no one was there, so I walked on. I think I must have stopped to poke my nose in a dozen places that day, and I concluded that Anshun was a town meant to be taken slow and on foot. The streets were lined with such a confusing array of open-air markets, I thought I would get lost. But almost all the buildings were two-storey wooden structures, and I was able to keep myself oriented with occasional glimpses of the stone pagoda at the south end of the old part of town.

Eventually, that was where I ended up, and I thought I might as well check out the pagoda. It was surrounded by a maze of walls and houses, and I asked an old lady how to get there. She just shrugged. But three children overheard my question, and they said they knew the way. They were only about eight years old, and their faces and clothes were covered with coal dust. They clearly knew every inch of their neighborhood. I followed them through a labyrinth of alleys, up a wall, across a

Anshun's stone pagoda

couple of roofs, dangerously close to some power lines, and finally up the hill's steep slope to the pagoda on top.

The pagoda was about ten meters high and constructed out of white granite. It had six sides, on each of which was a carving of a different buddha. There wasn't any path leading there, and the pagoda was clearly not yet ready for inclusion on the tourist circuit. According to local records, it was built by a monk in 1326, and it was rebuilt in 1851. There wasn't anything else on the hill, except a couple of trees waiting for spring, so I headed back down, this time through a building site. The foreman saw me and waved me through, but he made the three children go back the way they came. I waved goodbye. My eight-year-old guides doubtlessly could have shown me the whole town, but I had an appointment at the factory that produced Anshun's most famous product: indigo batik.

It was only a few blocks from the pagoda, and I was right on time. I had called earlier from my hotel, and they were expecting me. Well, sort of expecting me. That is to say, they were there, and so was I. As I walked through the front gate, the guard directed me to the reception room. And a few minutes later, the director of marketing came in. He had obviously just returned from a very long lunch. He was totally plastered and was having trouble standing without swaying. But he insisted on guiding me through the factory, him staggering onward and me leaning as far away as possible to keep from being overwhelmed by his breath. About all I had time to see was a workroom where a hundred women were dripping beeswax onto white cloth on which designs had already been printed. Before I could see the dying process, my guide collapsed and had to be helped away. I was relieved and took that opportunity to escape back out to the street.

But my indigo batik quest was not over. Anshun was smack-dab in the middle of Puyi country. It was the Puyi who supposedly first hit on the technique. Not far from Anshun was a place called Stone Village, and according to Puyi legend, there was once a girl who lived there who was famous for her dyed cloth. One day a bee landed on some of her undyed cloth, and she shooed it away. Later, when she dyed the cloth,

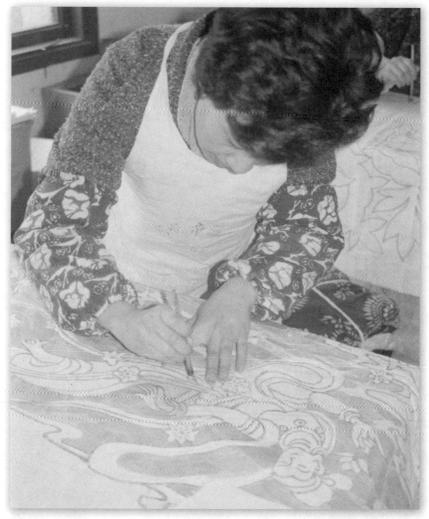

Worker applying wax to batik design

there was a small white spot where the bee had landed. She put two and two together and discovered the process that a hundred women were still following two thousand years later at the Anshun General Batik Factory, cranking out 1.5 million yards' worth of the stuff in 1991 alone, the year before my visit.

Huangkuoshu Falls

布依族

11. The Puyi

IN ADDITION TO having a certain urban charm in the older parts of town, Anshun was also the jumping-off point for several popular destinations, one of which was the most famous waterfall in China, Huangkuoshu Falls. From Anshun it was only forty-five kilometers on one of the best roads in the province through a landscape of limestone hills and Puyi villages. I couldn't resist. The next morning, I headed for the waterfall.

According to Puyi legend, a long, long time ago there was an evil landlord who married a beautiful young girl, and after a year she gave birth to a daughter. But then the landlord decided he liked another woman better, and he forced his wife to jump into the Paishui, or White-water River. But when she did, she turned into a magpie. Later, her daughter grew up and fell in love with a young shepherd boy, and they decided to run off together. They went down to the Paishui and built a raft and started paddling downstream. But someone saw them and told her father, and he and all his henchmen went down to the river and started paddling after the couple in eight boats. Before long, one of the landlord's boats was only a few feet behind. But just then, the girl's magpie mother swooped down and gave her daughter seven feathers, which turned into magic hairpins, and she told her daughter to throw one of the hairpins behind her raft. Her daughter did as she was told, and a chasm appeared in the river, and the pursuing boat disappeared into a watery grave. Each time another boat approached, the same thing happened, until only her father's boat was left. This time, since her daughter had no more magic hairpins, the magpie threw herself into the river. A bottomless chasm opened up once again and swallowed her former husband's boat, and the young couple lived happily ever after. And that was how Huangkuoshu and the other waterfalls along the Whitewater River came to be. In a little more than an hour, I was there.

After checking into the Huangkuoshu Guesthouse, which was the only hotel near the falls, I ate an early lunch and followed the other tourists down a trail that led to the river. Huangkuoshu Falls was named for a huge banyan-like huangkuo tree that was growing at the edge of the falls when it was first discovered by Chinese travelers back in the Ming dynasty. Among those early travelers was China's greatest travel diarist, Hsu Hsia-k'o, and it didn't take long for his account to attract others to the falls. Nowadays, hundreds of people visit every day, and it has become known as China's greatest waterfall. I'm not sure why it has been given that distinction. At seventy meters, it isn't China's highest waterfall, and a lot more water goes over Hukou Falls on the Yellow River. But it was a grand sight, and one that travelers could view not only from above and from below but also from behind. It turned out that the trail continued up into a limestone cave behind the falls that extended from one side to the other, and there were six openings where visitors could stand a few feet, or if they preferred, a few inches, from its curtain of thunder. There were so few tourists, I decided to spend the day there, which is something I almost never do on my travels. Back in my room, I even took a nap and then returned to the falls again to watch the sunset turn its spray a rainbow of colors. Later that night, lying in bed, I listened to the sound until I fell asleep.

The next morning, the thunder was still there. Huangkuoshu, though, was only one of eight waterfalls within a few kilometers of each other. Four of the eight, including Huangkuoshu, were nearby along the Whitewater River, and a fifth was a few kilometers to the south where the Whitewater became the Sancha River. The fifth was called Yinlien, or Silver Necklace, Falls. It was not as big as the others, but it was located in the middle of the Tienhsingchiao Water Wonderland, which the desk clerk at the hotel raved about, and I felt impelled to see what that meant.

There was a public bus that went to Tienhsingchiao about once an hour, depending on how long it took to fill up. It was also possible to hitch a ride with one of the tour groups that stopped at Huangkuoshu before continuing on to Tienhsingchiao. But since it was a fine day I decided to walk and took the road that wound south from the guesthouse. After about ten minutes, I saw a small sign on the left pointing down the mountain to the village of Huashihhsiao. Although the sign didn't say so, the path was also the shortcut to Tienhsingchiao, and I started down the stone steps. A few minutes later, I arrived at the Puyi village of Huashihhsiao.

As in other Puyi villages, all the houses were made of stone. The roofs were stone, too, large slabs of slate. The appearance was totally different from that of the other minority villages I had visited, where the houses were made of wood and built on stilts. Still, the same rule of etiquette applied. I sat down beneath a huge huangkuo tree at the edge of the village and waited to be invited.

While I waited, I took out a book I had bought at the guesthouse and read about the Puyi. The word "pu," it said, meant "man," and the name Puyi meant Tribe of Man. As of 1990, there were 2.5 million members living in China, with the major concentration in the southern half of Kueichou. Unlike the Miao, the Yao, and the Tung, whose ancestral homelands can be traced back to the fertile valleys of the Yangtze River or the Yellow River, the Puyi are living where they have always lived. None of their myths mention other places. Still, nobody knows how long the Puyi have lived here. Two thousand years ago, the Chinese referred to all the tribes south of their control as the Paiyueh, or Hundred Outsiders, and the Puyi were among them, as were the Chuang, whom I had already visited in Kuanghsi.

The Puyi aren't too clear themselves about their ancestry, and different villages tell different stories, but they all agree that their earliest ancestor was Pu-ling. In the Puyi language "pu-ling" means "man-ape," suggesting Darwin was a latecomer in linking man with his hairier cous-

Puyi village of Huashihhsiao

ins. According to the Puyi, a long time ago two rocks collided, and
the spark they produced gave birth to Pu-ling, who created everything
out of different parts of his body. It was an odd creation: for example,
Pu-ling pulled out all his hair and threw it on the ground, and each hair
gave birth to a human being. But Pu-ling didn't stop with his hair. He
cut off his feet and made mountains and cut off his fingers and made
trees. Flowers grew from his ears, and birds flew out of his nose, and
his entrails turned into rivers and seas. Pu-ling kept cutting until the
only parts left were his right hand, his tongue, and his heart. He then
threw down his heart, and his heart gave birth to the simian Lei-ling, the
ancestor of the Puyi people. His right hand flew up to the moon, where
it turned into a tree that is visible when the moon is full, and his tongue
turned into a rainbow that you can still see drinking after a rain.

Pu-ling, the man-ape, then disappeared from the scene, leaving Lei-
ling, the little monkey, in charge. But it was a wild world, and Lei-ling
taught the body-hair tribes how to make bows and arrows to protect
and feed themselves and how to strike rocks together to make fire to
cook and to keep warm. And that is the story of how things came to be.

It is all there in a three-thousand-line song the Puyi people sing whenever they celebrate the world's annual rebirth in spring.

Since it was early March, I was a few weeks too late for the spring festival but not too late to enjoy a little Puyi hospitality. Not long after I sat down outside the village of Huashihhsiao and read about how the Puyi came to be, an old couple came by on their way back from their fields and invited me to their home for a bowl of tea.

As with all the other houses in the village, the outside was made of stone, but the interior was made of wood. In a landscape where forests had long since been replaced with terraced fields, stone was cheap, and wood was expensive, and its use in homes was restricted to the interiors. Unlike in the wooden houses I had visited in Chuang, Yao, Tung, and Miao villages, there was no fire pit in the floor for cooking or for guests to warm their hands around. The kitchen was in a separate room with a stove made out of adobe bricks and where my hosts heated up some water for tea. While I waited, I noticed a pair of coffins in the open attic. Like the Miao, the Puyi aren't happy if they don't get their coffins ready before they die.

This was obviously a well-off couple, and they weren't all that far from a Chinese town, but the wife was dressed in a traditional Puyi jacket. It was strikingly different from the minority clothing I had seen up until then. First, the embroidery was different. The wife had adorned her jacket with masses and waves of the stuff, instead of the intricate geometry preferred by the Miao or the Yao. Then there was the batik. According to the Chinese, the Puyi not only produced the finest batik in China, they invented it. Whether or not that was true, Puyi batik was in a class of its own. One of the reasons their batik textiles were so beautiful was that the Puyi knew how to use dyes—not synthetic dyes like those used in the factories in Anshun, but natural dyes. And among these, indigo reigned supreme. In fact, indigo played a special role in Puyi culture.

For example, when a boy wants to marry a girl, he sends her a gift of indigo. If she accepts, she sends back a bolt of homespun cotton cloth printed with her most beautiful beeswax design and dyed with the boy's

Puyi clothing drying in Huashihhsiao

indigo. My host's jacket was a lovely example, with large patches of batik on the sleeves featuring a series of huge whorls. It was so impressive, I ended up buying it. My minority clothing collection already took up half my bag, and I had yet to figure out what I was going to do with it all. I suppose I will give it to my daughter someday, someday when a boy sends her some indigo or colored thread.

Finally, the water boiled, and my hosts brought me a big bowl infused with tea leaves into which they dropped a lump of rock sugar. That was new, the sugar. It was a welcome change—quick energy. Hot sugar water was the favorite drink of the hermits I had met in China's mountainous regions, if they could afford it. Usually they saved it for guests.

The village of Huashihhsiao was only a thirty-minute walk from the flood of tourists that inundated Huangkuoshu Falls every day, but it was in another world. A hundred people lived in the village, and they all supported themselves by farming and fishing. If they grew or caught more than they could eat, they considered themselves lucky. But they certainly knew how to enjoy themselves when they were lucky. No tribe in China has been credited with more drinking songs than the Puyi. They aren't like Western drinking songs about bottles of beer on the wall, but involve a dialogue of humility and flattery that alternates between the host and guest. At the Huangkuoshu Guesthouse I also bought a book of such songs translated into Chinese, just in case, and I've translated a small part of one into English to give an idea of how they go.

First the host sings: "Our house hides in a deep ravine / we have no wine to wet your throat / our house sits on a rocky cliff / we have no wine to honor guests / regrets, regrets, our deep regrets / it's so hard to lift our heads."

And the guest answers: "Your family is rich and big / your house is grand, your pigs are fat / the wine you brew is known to all / and now it fills our cups / my thanks, my thanks, my deepest thanks / you treat your guests so well."

A song like this goes back and forth half a dozen times, sometimes with much longer refrains. Unfortunately, I didn't get a chance to use even one of the refrains I had memorized. I arrived between festivals, and all I got was tea. The tea wasn't bad, but my book didn't have any tea drinking songs, so I just sat there looking dumb, until my hosts said they had to go dig up more indigo.

Since the place where they planned to look was in the same direction I was heading, I joined them and hiked down the mountain to the river. Along the way I passed their terraced fields. It was March and still too early for summer crops, but a third of the fields were full of winter wheat and green beans and rapeseed, from which they would be making cooking oil. Harvest, they said, was less than a month away. My Puyi hosts were carrying a mattock and a long iron rod to dig up indigo roots. Without any prodding on my part, they said their farm tools also served as weapons.

We continued down the mountain onto the road that followed the river. It looked safe enough, but my hosts said there were bandits in the surrounding mountains. I looked skeptical, but to make their point that they lived beyond the reach or protection of the law, the husband said he and his wife had four children, three sons and a daughter, and all of them born since Beijing decreed one child per couple. Clearly, in the land of the Puyi, Heaven was far away.

Finally, my hosts said goodbye and waded across the river. While they headed off across the adjacent ridge, I continued on. A few minutes later, I rounded a bend in the road and entered the parking lot of Tienhsingchiao Park. Earlier, my Puyi hosts had told me their family used to own the entire area encompassed by the park, but it was confiscated by the government during the Cultural Revolution. Bandits weren't only in the hills.

After paying the entrance fee, I entered what turned out to be an amazing landscape of water and rocks and trees. After the government confiscated the land from the villagers, it diverted water from the Sancha River so that it flowed through this area of oddly shaped limestone formations that were covered with banyans and several kinds of cacti, including agave and something that looked like prickly pear but without the prickles. A trail of stone steps led through this natural maze to

Silver Necklace Falls

another more open section of the park further downstream. After an hour or so of wandering, I finally arrived at Silver Necklace Falls.

I had already seen Huangkuoshu Falls and was duly impressed. But with buildings crowding it on both sides and a nice set of power lines above, it was grand but not beautiful. Silver Necklace was about one-twentieth the size, but it was like no waterfall I had ever seen: a watery necklace of intersecting, pearl-laden threads strung across the river goddess's black, moss-covered breasts. It was the most beautiful waterfall I had ever seen.

Despite such beauty, I eventually forced myself to continue on. There was more to Tienhsingchiao than met the eye. In fact, in some places I had to use my ears. Past the maze of rocks and trees and water that led visitors to Silver Necklace Falls, the trail led to another limestone area from which the park took its name: Tienhsingchiao, or Constellation Bridge, which was actually a calligrapher's mistake for Tienshengchiao, or Natural Bridge. Either way, it wasn't like any other bridge I had walked across before.

The bridge, if you could call it that, began where the Sancha River disappeared into an underground cavern, then flowed just below the surface in a one-kilometer-long limestone canyon before exiting again further downstream. Walking across the canyon floor, I could hear the river, but I couldn't see it. It reminded me of walking across the transparent black ice of a newly frozen lake when I was a boy in Idaho. Each step was a step of faith that the water wasn't as close as it looked, or, in this case, sounded. But when I walked across new ice, I always carried a pair of ice picks in my back pocket to pull myself out if the ice gave way. All I had this time was a flask of Canadian Club, to which I turned more than once.

After a few slugs, it wouldn't have mattered if the whole canyon floor gave way. In fact, my notes and recollection of Tienhsingchiao stop right there. All I remember was that Tienhsingchiao was, as advertised, a water wonderland. And it was well advertised. It was on the itinerary of most tour groups. And it was my good fortune that one of them was also taking in the water wonderland when I was there. The bus driver offered me a ride back to Anshun. He even stopped long enough at the guesthouse for me to collect my bag.

On the way back to Anshun, he told me that this was the first good job he had ever had. He was making the equivalent of 70 dollars a month. Before that, he said, life was tough. Forty years earlier, his father did a favor for the Kuomintang, and as punishment the government refused to let him or his brothers or sisters or even their children go to high school, much less college. They were all forced to do menial jobs. According to the driver, despite the window-dressing of economic reform, the goods hadn't changed. Success still depended on the right connections, and the right connections could just as easily turn out to be the wrong connections and a one-way ticket to Hell. The Chinese have certainly suffered during the past two hundred years at the hands of Western and Japanese imperialists, but only the Chinese really know how to abuse their fellow citizens.

Before returning to Anshun, the tour bus had one more stop to make, and I had no choice but to go along. After winding our way through a landscape of limestone hills, terraced fields of rapeseed in bloom, and the occasional Puyi village of stone huts, we arrived at a place called Lungkung, or Dragon Palace. From the parking lot, I joined the other members of the tour and followed a path up a hill to a small lake, where I boarded a metal boat. When there were about twelve of us in the boat, the boatman cast off and poled us all across the lake and into a cave, where a long time ago a Puyi maiden married a dragon who lived inside.

We lowered our heads to avoid the rocks that hung down from the roof near the entrance, and the boatman told us this story. A long time ago, there was a dragon who lived inside the cave, and he was the last of a long line of dragons. And because he was so lonely, he was also given to fits of rage, and he caused the people in the neighborhood no end of grief. Well, one day a beautiful, young Puyi girl came down to the lake to wash her soybeans in the water that flowed out of the dragon's cave. Normally, people avoided the lake, but she was young and a bit reckless, and while she was washing her soybeans, she slipped and fell into the lake and disappeared into the darkness below.

Several months later, she appeared to her parents in a dream and told them that after she fell into the lake she was rescued by the dragon, who took her inside his cave. After a brief courtship, she became his wife, and the dragon agreed not to cause the Puyi any more trouble. She told her parents not to worry, but she said there was something she needed. She asked her parents to bring her some soymilk. The next day just happened to be New Year's Day, and her parents went down to the lake and poured a huge container of soymilk into the water. Their daughter used the soymilk to suckle her dragon babies, and ever since then, the Puyi have come there at the beginning of every year and poured soymilk into the lake to make sure the local dragons send down enough rain for their crops.

As our boatman finished this story, we lifted our heads and found ourselves inside the Dragon Palace. The palace was made of a series of caverns. According to our boatman, they were fashioned into their present form by the dragon's Puyi wife. He said the underground river flowed through ninety similar caverns, but only the first few were open to the public.

After passing through the entrance, we drifted into a huge limestone chamber lit with colored neon lights. The effect was somewhat garish, and more thought could have gone into the placement of the lights. In fact, indirect lighting would have been better. But it was still an impressive sight, and the feeling that came from drifting through the underground cavern on that blackest of rivers was truly eerie. A dragon would certainly have been at home.

Altogether we passed through half a dozen such caverns for a distance of eight hundred meters, only one-fifth of the underground section of the river. Then the boatman poled us back the way we had come. The round-trip didn't take more than forty minutes. But it was a memorable forty minutes. Just outside the entrance, the river emptied into another cavern, turned into a waterfall, and flowed through the park at the foot of the mountain. On our way out, we sat down and enjoyed a Kueichou specialty: slices of potato and dried tofu that you fry yourself on a dome-shaped iron grill, then dip in a mixture of salt, anise, and red pepper. Delicious, especially with a dash of snowflakes and a shot of whiskey.

打鷄洞

12. Shuttlecock Cave

AFTER ANOTHER NIGHT at Anshun's Mintsu Hotel, I was off again. I had already visited the sights to the south. My destination this time was to the north, and it was another cave. Actually, it wasn't just another cave. It was Tachitung, or Shuttlecock Cave. Geologists at the Academy of Chinese Sciences claimed it was the best-preserved limestone cave in the world. They also said it was the world's most beautiful limestone cave, which was an odd claim for geologists to make.

I thought I would find out for myself and caught the early-morning bus from the central bus station. The bus was bound for Chihchin, the county seat about twenty kilometers from the cave. Buses also left from Anshun's north station, but the buses at the central station had cushioned seats, I was told, instead of vinyl-covered boards, and it was a long ride on a bad road.

The bad part wasn't long in coming. About an hour north of town, we pulled up behind a long column of buses and trucks and tractors. The road ahead was blocked, ironically, by an accident involving the north station's early-morning bus to Chihchin. We joined the crowd at the scene. It wasn't hard to tell what had happened. The bus was rounding a bend when it hit a truck loaded with coal coming around the same bend on the wrong side of the road. The head-on collision sent the bus careening into a nearby field. The truck simply crumpled and dumped its load of coal onto the road. I didn't see any bodies, but I didn't look too closely.

An hour later, a crew of road workers managed to clear a path through the wreckage and coal, and we began winding our way higher and higher into the mountains. As we did, no one fell asleep, which was what usually happened on long bus rides. Everyone seemed to be listening for the rumble of coal trucks. We also passed through a number of Puyi villages, and we stopped at one long enough to have more fried potatoes and tofu dipped in anise and red pepper, which the whole village turned out to watch me eat. Just below the summit of the road we were on, we stopped again, this time to fill the water reservoir on the bus's roof. There was a lever near the driver's seat that allowed him to control the flow from the reservoir onto the brakes, to keep them from burning up during the long descent into Chihchin, which we reached five hours after leaving Anshun—only an hour late.

Since Tachitung was still another twenty kilometers away, I walked from the long-distance bus station to the local bus station and caught the next leaves-when-it-fills-up bus to the cave. A few minutes later, I was back on another winding road. This one wound its way into the mountains east of Chihchin. Along the way, we passed hundreds of people on foot heading in the same direction. They were Miao, and it was market day, and the market they were all heading for turned out to be right in front of the cave. It took our bus ten minutes to honk its way through the crowd to the parking area in front of the cave entrance. The area wasn't only used for parking and the weekly market, it was also used as a sports field. And one of the favorite sports of the local children was kicking a shuttlecock into the air with their insteps. Apparently this had something to do with why they called the nearby hole in the mountain Tachitung, or Shuttlecock Cave. At least this was the bus driver's explanation, and it was good enough for me.

According to the sign at the entrance of the cave, the gate opened at nine in the morning and closed at six, and the tour took three hours. We arrived at three, just in time for the last tour of the day. Tickets were 15RMB, or 3 dollars, making it one of the more expensive entrance fees in China at the time. Even the Chinese had to pay 15RMB, which pretty much kept out the working class as well as the Miao and other ethnic minorities who once used the cave for religious ceremonies.

The group I arrived with consisted of the staff of the major provincial daily newspaper in Kueiyang. They were fellow journalists, fellow inmates in the Asylum of the Latest Breaking News, fellow parishioners in the Church of the Never-Ending Update. Insurance companies list journalists second only to air traffic controllers when it comes to suffering from stress, and I think Chinese journalists just might be ahead of air traffic controllers. After all, they have to report facts in a world where facts are not necessarily facts. One of Teng Hsiao-p'ing's favorite slogans was "Seek truth from facts." But in China truth is whatever the party wants it to be, and facts that veer from the party's version of truth are, in fact, not facts, and woe be the journalist who doesn't know the difference. I was glad to see the staff of the *Kueiyang Daily* taking a break from all this, although I couldn't help thinking it was ironic that they chose an underground cave for their day off. After a few minutes of waiting at the entrance, our guide showed up, and we entered what the Chinese call the biggest, best-preserved, most beautiful limestone cave in the world—and that's a fact.

Since Chinese authorities first learned about the cave twenty years earlier, they had created a three-kilometer-long underground trail so that tourists could see the world's biggest, best-preserved, and most beautiful limestone cave for themselves. The tour took anywhere from two to three hours, depending on how long your guide let you linger and how fast you walked. To make sure visitors didn't linger too long, all the lights in each cavern were linked to timers that left laggards in the dark when their guide moved on. During our tour, even the normally stoic Chinese were complaining about the pace. My own complaint wasn't so much the timers as it was the lighting itself. The bare neon tubes and cables didn't exactly complement China's most beautiful underground cave. And beautiful it was, as if this was where dead sculptors stayed while waiting to descend further underground. Some of them must have stayed a long time. They left behind just about every shape known, as if

Shuttlecock Cave

they had prolonged their plunge into the Netherworld by entertaining the Judge of Hell with their art. Ribbons hung down from the ceilings, columns spiraled up from the floor, and along the walls was a never-ending gallery of works that our guide likened to pagodas and trees and mushrooms and animals and vegetables. And was that the Bodhisattva of Compassion or Chairman Mao welcoming departed sculptors to this way station to the Underworld? Although this was one art gallery where photography was permitted, my camera was too fogged up to be of any use. But even if the air hadn't been too moist for normal photography, a thin layer of dust obscured much of the translucent beauty of the cave's limestone stalactites and stalagmites.

After our two-and-a-half-hour tour through the limestone wonderland, we returned to the world of daylight just as the sky was growing dark. The last bus back to Chihchin had already left, and the other members of my group filed into the hotel near the cave entrance. But I had my heart set on a night in Chihchin and an early-morning bus back to Anshun. So I passed the cave hotel by and walked down to what remained of the weekly market. About twenty Miao villagers were packing their goods and themselves into the back of an old truck. The driver said he was headed for Chihchin, and he waved for me to climb aboard. Someone reached down and helped me up. I kicked an old lady in the head as I got in, but she just laughed and handed me a baked potato. A few minutes later, we were bouncing down the mountain, screaming like a bunch of kids every time the truck hit a bump. Miraculously, no one fell off.

Forty minutes later, I was back in Chihchin. Riding in the back of an old Liberation truck with a bunch of Miao villagers and their produce was so much fun, it was with sadness that I lowered myself back down to the ground and waved goodbye and went to look for a hotel. In Chihchin, foreigners were supposed to stay at the hotel next to the county government building. But it was two kilometers from where the truck dropped me off, and I managed to convince the desk clerk at the government hostel across the street from the bus station that I was too tired to make it that far and it was okay for me to stay there, just for the night.

After dropping my bag in my room, I went back outside and ate dinner at a small restaurant two doors down the street. The cook made me a big plate of fried potatoes and dried tofu. Only this time, instead of the usual anise and red peppers, he poured on some kind of steak sauce. It was so good, I broke down and had my first beer in a week. Later, back at the hotel, I joined several other guests and soaked away the bumps of the road in a communal bathtub the size of my hotel room. It had been a few years since I had been in a bath like that. When I first started traveling in China, every town had a communal bath, and most towns had several. They didn't just provide travelers and locals alike with a place to bathe, they provided a place for socializing, a place to review the events of the day, if not the week. I would have joined in the talk, but the dialect was beyond me, so I just soaked.

It had been a long day, and as soon as I returned to my room and lay down, I was asleep. That was another function of the communal bath. It provided the opportunity for a much longer soak than a small bathtub. It was a good thing I decided to set my alarm clock. I slept for nine hours, and would have slept for a few more. I made it across the street to the bus station just in time to catch the seven o'clock heading south back to Anshun. The ride hardly compared to that of the previous day. In fact, it was so boring, I fell asleep.

草海

13. Tsaohai Lake

I T WAS NOON when I arrived back in Anshun. Over the previous few days, I had visited the sights east of Anshun, south of Anshun, and north of Anshun. It was time to go west, and the next major town to the west was Liupanshui. There was a daily bus. But by the time I got to the right bus station, it had already left. My only option was the train. But by the time I made it to the train station, I was too late for the morning and midday trains. My only option was the evening express. After buying a ticket, I went back to the Mintsu Hotel and rented a room for the afternoon. I decided to take a break. I lounged in my room and caught up in my journal and made it back to the train station with time to spare.

Despite originating the previous day in Kuangchou 1,500 km to the east, the train was only five minutes late. I could see why. It didn't stop long. Still, it was somehow long enough for me and a few thousand other passengers to squeeze on. There were no seats, but I managed to find enough room between cars for my pack, and despite the crush of bodies, at least I was able to sit down. A few minutes later, the conductor came through checking tickets and offered me something even better—a berth.

It was wonderful the way train personnel on Chinese trains looked after foreigners. I knew it was partly because they didn't want to deal with the problems that might occur when foreigners got their pockets picked, but it was also out of genuine concern. This was especially true in the Southwest, where trains were few and so were foreigners. I thanked the conductor but turned down the berth. Liupanshui was only two and a half hours away. And we arrived there right on schedule at ten thirty.

Liupanshui was a coal-mining, steel-milling town, and it gave the impression of being a wild place. At most train stations, disembarking passengers could only leave by passing through a gate where their tickets were checked one last time. But at Liupanshui, my train was met by a dozen touts from local "hotels." Since it was late, I decided not to waste time looking for a place of my own choosing. I followed one of the touts across the tracks, through a hole in the fence, and down an alley to a private home that served just fine as a place to spend the night.

Along with the town of Kaili in the eastern part of the province, and the capital of Kueiyang in the middle, Liupanshui rounded out Kueichou's industrial nightmares. One-third of the province's coal came from the hills surrounding Liupanshui, and much of that was used to stoke a dozen nearby steel mills. But I wasn't there to witness China's version of the Industrial Revolution. I was hoping to see one of the world's rarest birds, the black-necked crane, whose black neck didn't come from Liupanshui's coal soot. As soon as I woke up the next morning, I asked my host to direct me to the local bus station. It was only ten minutes away, and once there I only had to wait five minutes before leaving for the town of Weining eighty kilometers to the northwest. Weining was the home of the Tsaohai Nature Reserve, which was the home of the black-necked crane and a dozen other rare birds.

I was only too glad to leave Liupanshui's muddy streets behind. The mud was from the snow that had been falling off and on for the previous few days and was now melting. And the snow and the mud were now joined by fog. As we wound our way through the mountains to the north, we passed a truck that had gone over the edge a few minutes earlier and had careened down the slope into a wheat field thirty meters below the road. Miraculously, the driver wasn't hurt, although he did look dazed. Our driver stopped long enough for the man to write down a message to give to someone in Weining before continuing on through the fog.

The people of Kueichou province have a saying: "Where is the person with three ounces of silver? Where is the place with three hectares of flat land? And where is the sky that stays blue for three days? Not in Kueichou." Obviously, that saying isn't popular with the Kueichou tourist authorities, but it is true, especially the last part about the sky. Halfway to Weining, though, as the bus I was on crossed a mountain ridge, for the first time since I had begun traveling in Kueichou, there was the sun. It was early morning, and the fog was just lifting. The sun looked like it was coming out of hiding just behind the Yi village we passed as we headed down the mountain.

Next to the Miao, the Yi are Kueichou's largest ethnic minority. The Yi say that a long time ago the world had no light, and people and animals lived their lives in darkness until Ssu-tzu Ti-ni, one of the gods responsible for creating the world, saw the suffering of the earth's creatures and sent A-lu Chu-tzu to provide the world with light. Well, A-lu Chu-tzu knew how to follow orders, and that was about all. He filled the sky with seven suns and nine moons. And after reporting that his mission was a complete success, he and Ssu-tzu Ti-ni went off to fix up another world.

Meanwhile, back on Earth, plants withered, rivers dried up, and people and animals alike had a hard time finding enough to eat or drink until the great Yi hero Chih-ko A-lung climbed to the top of a mountain and shot his magic arrows into the sky, killing six of the suns and eight of the moons. Unfortunately, the surviving sun and moon were so frightened, they went into hiding. It was only with great difficulty that they were enticed back into the sky, and they are still a little shy around places where the Yi live. And that is why the sky in Kueichou is rarely blue three days in a row.

But it was my good fortune to experience one such blue-sky day in the high plateau town of Weining, where we arrived just after passing the edge of a vast reed-filled lake. The lake was Tsaohai, Kueichou's famous Grass Sea, and the home of one of China's most unusual nature

Black-necked cranes at Tsaohai

reserves. From the bus station, I walked back toward the lake. It wasn't even a ten-minute walk, if that. Just before I reached the lake, I saw a building that turned out to house the Nature Reserve Headquarters, which looked out over the lake it was established to protect.

According to geologists, Tsaohai was formed over the past several million years from the water that flowed from the area's steadily rising mountain ranges. As a result of the uplifting of the surrounding mountains, the lake that formed was left with no outlet, and it became a haven for waterfowl. Then, about a hundred years ago, the Chinese decided the lake would make a great place to grow crops, and they tried to drain it. Over the past century, they had tried to drain it eight times, most recently during the Cultural Revolution. Local records say each attempt was followed by hailstorms and droughts and plagues of locusts, and still the authorities persisted.

Finally, with the end of the Cultural Revolution, the provincial government agreed to restore the lake to its natural state. That was in 1980. Five years later the government turned over control of the lake to the province's new Environmental Protection Administration, and seven years later I walked through their front gate. The lobby of the main building, such as it was, was empty, but down one of the corridors, I met Mr. Ch'en, the director. I was surprised to see a nature reserve so close to an urban center, and I asked Mr. Ch'en about the effect the town had on the lake's wildlife. He admitted there were problems involving pollution and encroachment. But he said that since the lake had been turned into a nature reserve, it had attracted back most of the wildlife that had lived there before the last time it was drained.

Mr. Ch'en said that he had no previous experience in the area of environmental protection. He had worked earlier for the county government. But the solution, he said, to the problems involving factories and farms required assistance from other branches of the local government, and he had close ties with all of them. In fact, the new offices of the county government were going up right across from the Nature Reserve Headquarters. I guess they couldn't pass up the view.

Despite his lack of environmental experience, Mr. Ch'en was visibly excited about his job, and he led me through an exhibition room full of stuffed birds. He said more than a hundred species lived around the lake, and more than forty of those spent their winters there. Among the latter was the black-necked crane, which had led me there in the first place. The black-necked crane spent summers and autumns in Chinghai province, near the source of the Yellow River. Unfortunately, I ended my trip to the source of the Yellow River a bit too early the previous year to see any cranes. When I mentioned this to Mr. Ch'en, he offered to remedy my earlier omission and waved for me to follow him down to the lake.

A few minutes later, we boarded a small skiff, and he and one of his assistants began poling us from the shore through a long canal and into the reserve. Most nature reserves were themselves protected by some sort of buffer area. But the Tsaohai reserve was bordered by a large town and thousands of small farm plots—the remnants of the last attempt to drain the lake for farmland.

Mr. Ch'en said that when the government established the nature reserve in 1985, it set aside an area of twenty-five square kilometers, of which twenty consisted of the lake itself, and the remaining five were marshland. As we worked our way through the marshland, we turned into an adjacent canal, and the director told me not to move. A pair of black-necked cranes were standing in a field less than thirty meters away. The boatman continued to pole us in their direction. The black-necked crane was one of the world's rarest birds—the rarest member of the crane family. Protection, though, had increased its numbers from several hundred to more than a thousand, one-third of which spent their winters at Tsaohai Lake. Earlier, Mr. Ch'en had told me that the head of the World Wildlife Federation had been there four times to see these birds. And there they were. Mr. Ch'en's assistant continued poling us closer, to within fifteen meters, then ten, then five, then they flew, slowly, elegantly. They circled around and passed right over our boat, so close that I could feel the wind from their wings. They were huge birds, with a white body and white primary feathers, black secondary feathers, and a black neck with a red patch between the eyes. Mr. Ch'en estimated their weight at over eight kilos, about twice the weight of the Canada geese I tried to hunt when I was boy. But I could never get close enough. Ducks weren't so lucky. One day when I was fourteen, I went berserk and shot twenty-four mallards, and we had to eat duck every day for a month. One of those black-necked cranes would have lasted us just as long. They were too close to miss. But this time I used my Nikon.

Afterwards, we ventured out into the lake itself. It only had an average depth of two meters, but it was fed by streams from the nearby mountains that kept the level fairly constant. Over the course of an hour, we also saw gray cranes and bar-headed geese and fire ducks. But after the black-necked cranes, the rest was anticlimactic. Finally, Mr. Ch'en's assistant poled us back to shore, and I thanked them both for such a rare excursion. Mr. Ch'en said next time I should get a permit. The nature reserve wasn't open to tourists, and foreigners were supposed to contact the local office of foreign affairs to arrange a visit. As usual, I had simply stumbled in. Fortunately, the director turned out to be an enthusiastic guide and willing to overlook a little red tape. He invited me back for a longer stay and added that the nature reserve had a small hostel for visitors. I promised to return with a permit next time and walked back to the middle of town.

The last bus to Liupanshui was due to leave at two o'clock, and I was just in time. I could have spent the night in Weining, I suppose. But I wanted to get back so that I could catch the night train to Kunming, which the Chinese call the City of Eternal Spring. Ever since arriving in Kueichou, I had seen nothing but rain and snow and clouds. One day of sunshine convinced me I had to have more, and so I headed back to Liupanshui and the train line that hopefully would lead me from winter to spring.

It was a much less stressful trip than earlier. The fog was gone. Also, halfway to Liupanshui the bus stopped for gas in a small town where it was market day. Among the handicrafts for sale were bongs made from bamboo. I assumed they were for tobacco and not marijuana. The market was full of turbaned men and women decked out in long embroidered robes. They were Miao, more specifically Tahua Miao, or Big Flower Miao. We didn't stay long enough for me to examine their embroidery, but one foreigner who did was Samuel Pollard. He was a Christian missionary who came here at the end of the nineteenth century. He used the embroidery patterns woven by the Miao women in the Weining area to create a Miao script. He then had Bibles and hymnals printed with the new script, and he distributed these throughout the province. It was an ingenious script and remained in use even after the Communist takeover. Unfortunately, I didn't stay long enough to find out if anyone still used it.

As soon as we were gassed up, we continued on and made it back to Liupanshui a bit after five o'clock. When I went inside the train station to get a ticket for the night express, the only ticket I could buy was one that guaranteed me nothing more than a place to stand, which was normal, as tickets that promised a berth were usually reserved for party or government officials. The station attendant who sold me the ticket, though, did what she could to make my wait a pleasant one. First, she directed me to the station employees' shower, where I washed away

Tobacco bongs for sale at Tahua Miao village

the dust of the road. Then, when I was done, she led me to the station hostel, where I lay down in comfort and woke up just in time to catch the night train to Kunming. Again, I felt like I was being looked after by the gods.

As the ten-thirty express pulled into the station, though, the gods were nowhere to be seen. There was an incredible scramble by hundreds of people to get on during the two minutes the train was scheduled to stop. This was the express from Kuangchou again, and it had no intention of lingering in a town like Liupanshui. Fortunately, the wave of people behind me carried me into one of the cars. Obviously, there weren't any seats. But I didn't want a seat anyway. I was after a bed. Kunming was more than eight hours away, and the train wasn't due to arrive until the next morning. One thing all train travelers in China learn sooner or later is that even though stations might not sell tickets for berths, berths are often available on board on a first-come, first-sleep basis. The question is where to get in line. The answer is usually the car next to the dining car. Since the express was pulling over twenty cars, before it arrived I had asked one of the station employees where the dining car was likely to be when the train pulled in. The dining car was used to divide the sleeper section from the rest of the train, and without a sleeper ticket, you couldn't get through the dining car. But at one end of the car next to the dining car was a booth. Once the train was rolling, the conductor walked back to that booth, and if berths were available, that was where you got them. And on this occasion, when the conductor came back to hand out berths, I was first in line. Not only were berths available, there was even one in the soft sleeper section. It was a little expensive at 90RMB, or 17 bucks, but thefts, cigarette smoke, and late-night soirees were common problems in the hard sleeper section, and I wanted to arrive in Kunming rested and with all of my belongings. And so the gods welcomed me to the City of Eternal Spring.

昆明

14. Kunming

I WOKE UP IN Yunnan. I was south of the clouds at last. When the train staff came through and rousted us all out of bed, it was six o'clock in the morning, and there wasn't a single puff of white in the sky. While I was trying to come to grips with the day, one of the train workers told me that she first started working on the Kuangchou-Kunming line back in 1965. She said Kunming was nothing but rice fields and shacks then. I knew she wasn't exaggerating. When he visited Kunming in 1930, Edgar Snow found it "filthy, frustratingly inefficient, and dangerously barbaric." The man who later brought China's Communist movement to the attention of the world in *Red Star over China* said he "was shocked, but fascinated, to find a city unchanged in so many ways for a thousand years despite being closely connected with the civilized world by railway since the turn of the century." Snow was referring to the line built by the French from Hanoi and not the one I was arriving on.

Times had changed. As I stepped out of the station and boarded a local bus to the hotel of my choice, there was no doubt in my mind I had arrived in the cleanest, most efficient, most modern city in Southwest China. The streets were boulevards, and they were lined with sidewalks as wide as the streets in some of the cities I had visited days earlier. Instead of featuring claptrap hovels and dreary, look-alike buildings all the same color despite being different colors, Kunming was filled with structures that looked like they had been designed by somebody other than the local party chief's son-in-law. Just as the sun was rising, I checked into one of them, the memorable Camellia Hotel.

Kunming was full of new joint-venture hotels involving foreign hospitality firms, but the Camellia was easily the best value, especially the rooms in the old wing, where a double went for 50RMB, or 9 dollars. For a Chinese city, Kunming wasn't that old. It only dated back seven hundred years. But it was built between two sets of hills the Chinese had heard about thousands of years earlier.

The story began three thousand years ago in North China during the Chou dynasty when the heir to the Middle Kingdom's throne possessed two marvelous creatures, a golden horse that could fly and a jade phoenix that could dance and sing. During the day the jade phoenix entertained the princess, while the prince rode the golden horse into the clouds to inspect his father's realm. Often, though, the prince didn't come home until quite late. And when he did, he brought back young women whom he had rescued from one rascal or another and added them to his own ever-growing staff of female attendants. The prince told his wife he was just being chivalrous. Naturally, she thought otherwise. And one night, after the prince had gone to bed, the princess decided to put an end to her husband's gallivanting.

It seems that the horse's power of flight came from a magic bridle. So while the prince was asleep, the princess slipped the magic bridle over the horse's head and slapped its behind. Just as the horse reared up, the jade phoenix saw its chance to escape as well. It jumped onto the horse's back, and the two creatures sailed into the clouds and never returned to North China. Instead, they flew south and finally came down on the two hills on either side of what is now Kunming. In honor of that miraculous event, the people who lived here named the hill to the east Golden Horse Hill and the hill to the west Jade Phoenix Hill, and they built temples on both. That was a long time ago, and the names of the hills have changed, but people still visit the shrines on their slopes, and I decided to join them.

The receptionist at the hotel told me Golden Horse Hill, or Songbird Hill as it was now called, was a short bus ride away. But she added that it was a long climb to the Taoist temple near the summit. The temple's shrine hall was made completely of copper, three hundred tons of it, and there was a six-hundred-year-old camellia tree at the temple that would have been in bloom about then. Despite the lure of such attractions, I didn't feel like a long hike and decided instead to head for the hill where the jade phoenix landed. Nowadays people call it West Hill, because it is west of the city. Or they call it Sleeping Beauty Hill, because from a distance it looks like a reclining woman, complete with flowing hair.

From downtown Kunming, I took a bus that dropped me off twenty minutes later halfway up West Hill in front of Huating Temple. It was the largest Buddhist temple on the mountain, and outside the gate were two huge, wrathful-looking figures mounted on dragons. Their names were Heng and Ha, and their story went back to the Shang dynasty more than three thousand years ago. Heng and Ha were two generals in the service of the Shang emperor, and they both possessed supernatural powers. Heng destroyed his enemies by snorting flames of burning fire from his nostrils, while Ha destroyed his enemies by blowing streams of poison gas from his mouth. Despite possessing such powers, they were killed by a rival state that succeeded in overthrowing the Shang and setting up the Chou dynasty. The new rulers decided to honor these two generals by conferring upon them the status of protectors of the realm—a status Buddhists later appropriated for their temples. The figures of Heng and Ha standing outside Huating Temple were considered the finest in all of China. Children, I noticed, tended to run past them. I didn't linger either.

Just beyond them, I entered the temple's initial shrine hall and was welcomed by equally huge statues of the Four Guardians. Despite their presence in Buddhist shrine halls in China, the origin of these figures was connected with the Hindu religion. Soon after Indra created the universe, he assigned these guardians to protect the four quarters of the world, and in the T'ang dynasty an Indian monk named Amogha introduced them to the Chinese as worthy of veneration. Amogha was a proponent of a Buddhist sect closely linked with Hinduism, namely the Tantric sect, and among his disciples were the Chinese emperor and the

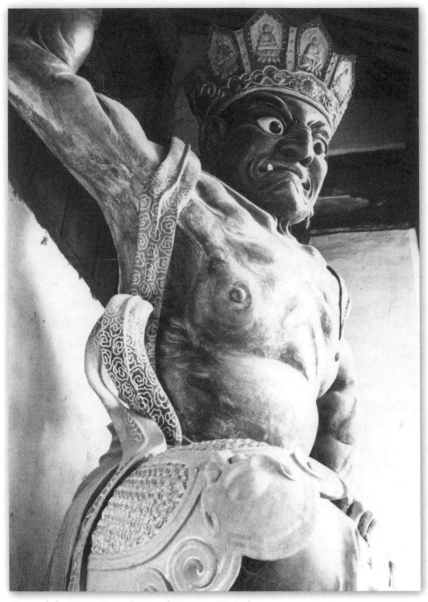

One of the Four Guardians of Hauting Temple

The Five Hundred Arhats at Huating Temple

crown prince. Before long, the Four Guardians were protecting temples throughout China, and they had been protecting the one on West Hill for the past nine hundred years.

Beyond the wrathful Heng and Ha and the Four Guardians, I crossed an open courtyard and entered the temple's main shrine hall. It was a huge, wooden-beamed hall whose walls from the floor to the ceiling were lined with a wonderful array of statues of that wild and crazy bunch of Buddhist guys known as the five hundred arhats. "Arhat" is a Sanskrit word that refers to the fourth and final stage of the Buddhist path, namely, freedom from passion and thus rebirth. In modern Mandarin, "arhat" is pronounced "lo-han," or "a-lo-han," and if you are ever in a Chinese restaurant and want a vegetarian dish, you can always order "lo-han-tsai," the arhat plate.

Meanwhile, back to the arhats, specifically the group of five hundred. Each member of this group possessed some special power or performed some miraculous deed during their lifetime, and it was fun, if not instructive, to see how Chinese artists interpreted the stories associated with individual members. There weren't any signs with their names, but it was easy to spot the two arhats whose legs and arms started growing and kept growing until they were able to grab the sun and moon out of the sky, or the arhat who ripped open his stomach to reveal a pagoda inside, or the arhat whose eyebrows hung down to the floor. This was an especially good group, and I would have lingered, but there was more to see up the road.

I continued uphill and thirty minutes later came to Taihua Temple. Taihua was built in 1306, three hundred years after Huating Temple, and it was not as large. The gruesome statues of Heng the Snorter and Ha the Blower I had seen earlier at the entrance of Huating Temple were missing. The Four Guardians, though, were at their usual posts inside the gate. And beyond them was a courtyard full of ancient gingko trees and camellias and magnolias and even an ancient red cassia.

I paid what the guardians asked and walked around the courtyard, which was quite lovely. Then I entered the main shrine hall. A sign asked pilgrims not to light incense or candles. The sagging wooden beams suggested that unlike Huating Temple, Taihua hadn't been rebuilt since it was first constructed. The statues were different, too. At Huating the walls of the main hall were lined with the five hundred arhats. At Taihua there were only eighteen. The eighteen arhats, though, were a more select group, representing disciples of the Buddha who agreed to stay in this world to save others. Actually, this should have made them bodhisattvas (the exemplars of Mahayana Buddhism) rather than arhats (the exemplars of Hinayana Buddhism), but the monks often fuzzed the distinction in favor of not confusing the pilgrims. The pilgrims, meanwhile, couldn't have cared less. They were busy throwing coins at the bowl of fruit on the main altar. According to one of them, anyone whose coin landed in the bowl without bouncing out was assured of having their suffering reduced next life, if not this life. I tossed in a couple of coins myself, hoping it would help the next time I needed a seat or a berth on a train. Having divested myself of my spare change, I returned to the road and continued uphill once more.

Along the way, the road went past a set of steps that led into the nearby woods to the grave of Nieh Er. Nieh was a young Chinese musician who drowned in 1935 at the age of twenty-four while on holiday in Japan. Despite his youth, he was one of China's most famous composers, and one of his marching songs is still used as China's national anthem. After a brief visit to his grave, I returned to the road one last time and continued on until it came to an end a few minutes later. A long flight of steps led to Sanchingko, the Pavilion of Three Purities. In Taoism, the three purities refer to states of being known as jade purity, supreme purity, and ultimate purity. Every time I try to distinguish them, I get lost in a labyrinth of language and mystery. This time I didn't stay long enough, if only because there wasn't much there, except for some new statues that tried to put the arcana of Taoism's triple cultivation into human form.

The pavilion itself was actually a group of five or six structures strung across a cliff. When they were first built in the early fourteenth century, they were intended as a summer residence for a Mongol prince. The Mongols had just brought that part of Asia into their orbit, and the prince was in charge of their new Southwest territories. The pavilion was later taken over by Taoists, and now it belonged to tourists, whose heels I followed up a winding stone staircase that tunneled into the cliff face of Kunming's West Hill. Work on the staircase had begun two hundred years earlier when a Taoist monk who had nothing better to do decided to tunnel through the cliff to a rocky perch higher up. He died before reaching his goal, but his work was carried on by others. I squeezed my way through to the opening they had created just below the summit. This was Dragon Gate.

The old monk who began chiseling his way there was creating a path to separate higher beings from the ordinary school of fish. He called his path Lungmen, or Dragon Gate, in imitation of a gorge through which the Yellow River passed just before it turned east and headed across its floodplain toward the sea. Every spring Yellow River carp still fight their way through the gorge to reach spawning grounds upstream. Few make it, but the Chinese say that those that do become dragons. By analogy, anyone who managed to pass the imperial exams was likened to a carp that made it past Dragon Gate. Hence, to reward students who made it through that particular gate, a shrine was carved into this cliff honoring the God of Literature, who appeared in his original incarnation as the three-eyed star god K'uei Hsing, wielding a writing brush and riding a dragon. Students who climbed here to ask his assistance, however, should have looked closer. In addition to K'uei Hsing's brush, there was a book on which he had written the words, "Success depends on Heaven."

Since I had long ago given up taking exams or applying for jobs, I simply took in the view. The view from Dragon Gate across the wide blue waters of Tienchih Lake was the most famous view in the Kunming area and worth the climb. I sat down on a bench and felt the warmth of the sun on my face. It was such a rare treat after traveling through Kuanghsi and Kueichou, I stayed there for half an hour just enjoying the yellow sun and the blue water. Then I remembered I was a tourist, and there was more to see in Kunming, or at least in the Kunming area.

I worked my way back down from Dragon Gate to where city buses turned around, and caught the next one heading to town. I had one more temple to visit. It was called Chiungchussu, or Bamboo Cane Temple, and it was in the hills northwest of town. Buses left from in front of the Yunnan Hotel as soon as they were full, and an hour after I left Dragon Gate I was at Bamboo Cane.

A sign near the entrance recounted the temple's origin. It seems that one day two brothers went hunting in these hills for wild pigs and suddenly spotted a rhinoceros. In prehistoric times, rhinos were common throughout China, but the brothers spotted this rhino in 638 AD. By then rhinos were few and far between, and the two brothers followed the rhino with something akin to reverential awe until it disappeared into a clump of bushes.

A few seconds later, a group of monks walked out of the same bushes carrying bamboo canes, and as soon as they were clear of the bushes, they stuck their canes into the ground and vanished. That was too much for the brothers. They ignored the possibility that the rhino might still be in the bushes and walked over to where the monks had left their canes. When the brothers grabbed the canes, they couldn't pull them out of the ground, no matter how hard they tried. Finally, they gave up and went home. But they returned the next day to prove to themselves that they hadn't been dreaming. The canes were still there, but during the night they had sprouted leaves and multiplied to form a huge bamboo grove. The brothers took this for a sign and resolved to build a Buddhist temple on the site, a temple that I entered 1,354 years later. It was named after a kind of bamboo used since time immemorial to make canes. Nearly 2,200 years ago, one of China's earliest emissaries to the Western world found canes made from this bamboo for sale in what is now Afghanistan. His informants told him the bamboo came from the area now encompassed by the provinces of Yunnan and Kueichou. There was a lot more than silk that traveled Central Asia's ancient Silk Road. But who would have expected bamboo canes from China's remote Southwest?

Once more I walked past the Four Guardians. As I stepped into the main courtyard, I found myself surrounded by galleries containing one of the artistic treasures of the Kunming area—another collection of the

Rhino door panels at Bamboo Cane Temple

five hundred arhats. I had already run into them at Huating Temple, but these were wilder and crazier, and they were life size and in better shape, which was to be expected considering they were only a hundred years old. Another unique feature was that each of these Buddhist worthies was riding something different: a dragon, a donkey, a fish, a crab, a turtle, a unicorn, even a black-necked crane.

After passing through the galleries, I walked into the main shrine hall and found an even more famous relic. It was a stone stele sent here by the emperor in 1316. His decree was carved in both Chinese and Mongol scripts and directed the temple's abbot to spread the Buddha's teachings among the barbarians. That was during the Yuan dynasty, when the Mongols ruled not only all of China but also parts of China that hadn't been parts of China before, including the region known as South of the Clouds.

Behind the main shrine hall, I climbed another series of steps to another shrine hall. Although clearly recent, the hall's workmanship was superb, if a bit unusual. Each of the hall's eight doors featured a carved panel of a rhino, some with one horn, some with two. That was the first time I had seen rhinos used as an artistic motif in China. But I shouldn't have been surprised. After all, it was a rhino that led the brothers who built the first version of the temple.

Moving past the rhinos, I entered the temple's final shrine hall. The artwork inside was as unexpected as the rhino panels earlier. Behind the buddha statue, a huge relief showed a procession led by the king who ruled this region when the temple was first built. He looked like Yul Brynner when he played the King of Siam in *The King and I*. Assuming the artists were somehow faithful to the period, the king was clearly not Chinese. He looked Thai, which was to be expected. The region known as South of the Clouds was still south of Chinese control back in the T'ang dynasty.

Having seen what there was to see, I headed back to Kunming on the next bus and made one more stop on my one-day tour of the capital. I went to the provincial museum to find out more about the region's ancient past, which apparently included Thai kings and rhinos. Unfortunately, a history of the creatures and cultures in this part of China had yet to be written. Until recently, Chinese historians dismissed their neighbors in the Southwest as barbarians. But the barbarians, it turns out, developed a civilization every bit as early and every bit as advanced as that of their overbearing neighbors to the north.

The Chinese had always assumed they were responsible for civilizing the Southwest and dismissed as legends stories about the area's ancient kings, especially those of other-than-Han ancestry. Given the absence of any written records, who could have argued that they weren't right? But archaeological evidence has now supplied what written records have failed to.

Past the first-floor exhibits of the province's current ethnic groups, I entered a wing on the second floor devoted to their ancestors. I ignored the stones and bones of prehistory and headed straight for the bronzes. A bronze was no easy thing to make, requiring large amounts of copper and tin ore that had to be mined. But over the previous four decades archaeologists had collected thousands of bronze implements and vessels from tombs in Yunnan dating back 3,200 years.

On previous trips, I had seen China's great bronze collections at the museums in Shanghai, Sian, and Wuhan, but Kunming's collection was unique. The earliest bronzes found in North China dated back 3,800 years, or about 600 years earlier than Yunnan's earliest bronzes. But archaeologists think Yunnan's bronze technology may have been introduced from somewhere other than China. The earliest bronzes found to date in the province were unearthed near the Burma border along an ancient trade route that connected Southeast Asia with Central Asia. Historians are now of the opinion that North China's own bronze technology was transmitted from the Middle East along Central Asian trade routes and that Yunnan may have benefited from this connection, though somewhat later. You may recall those bamboo canes from Yunnan that a Chinese emissary saw for sale in an Afghan market 2,200 years ago.

In any case, the metallurgists of Yunnan went their own way, favoring huge bronze drums over the ceremonial tripods of North China.

And instead of the stylized motifs and mythical beasts of their northern colleagues, they covered their bronzes with lifelike animals and realistic scenes. On one such bronze, a boar, a tiger, and a snake were locked in a never-ending fight to the death. Elsewhere, two bronze captives with their hands tied behind their backs dangled from the top of a bronze spear. The artist was even careful to include their testicles. Equally unforgettable was another captive being tortured on a primitive rack, his face twisted into a silent bronze scream. Maybe the Chinese were right. Maybe these people were barbarians. Whoever they were, they were people who knew how to make bronze, even if they left no written records, at least none that have survived.

They first appeared in Chinese records 2,100 years ago, when their ruler allied himself with the Chinese emperor and in recognition received a seal conferring on him the title King of Tien, which was the name of the huge lake I had viewed earlier from Dragon Gate. And the Chinese emperor called the king's subjects members of the Tien tribe. In the ensuing centuries, the Tien vanished from the scene and were replaced by other tribes, many with ancestral roots in Tibet and Szechuan as well as Vietnam and Burma. The region remained beyond Chinese control until the Mongols finally marched down and conquered it at the end of the thirteenth century. Yunnan was still a complex mixture of peoples. When I stopped on the first floor on my way out, I saw exhibits of clothing worn by members of twenty-four different ethnic groups and was told that the province included over fifty. I wasn't surprised so many people had settled here. There wasn't a cloud in the sky. And when the sun went down, I could see stars.

石林

15. Stone Forest

A MONG YUNNAN'S FIFTY ethnic groups, the third largest, after the Chuang and the Miao, are the Yi, with 6.5 million members. Among the Yi, the most famous, as well as the most accessible, is the branch known as the Sani, who live in and around Yunnan's most famous scenic wonder, the Lunan Stone Forest. There were hourly buses to Lunan from Kunming, but there was a more interesting way to get there. There was a train. It ran several times a day on the narrow-gauge railway built by the French at the beginning of the twentieth century between Kunming and Hanoi. How could I pass it up? But I didn't buy just one ticket. The ticket seller advised me to buy four. I thought maybe this was her way of commenting on my girth, but it wasn't. The seats were tiny, really tiny, and I ended up using all four—two for me and two for my gear.

As we rolled out of Kunming the next morning and through the Yunnan countryside, I once more found myself beneath a sunny sky. I hadn't seen the sun two days in a row since I left Hong Kong, which was now a distant memory. I was already looking forward to the third day in a row. When the conductor came through checking tickets and passports, he said the train continued all the way to the town of Hokou at the Vietnam border. Chinese could cross the border and continue on to Hanoi, but not foreigners.

I forgot to ask him how long it took to reach Hokou. I'm guessing all day. Most of the passengers brought along baskets of fruit and snacks.

The Stone Forest of Lunan

Those who didn't could choose from trays of bananas and peanuts and beer or order rice and vegetable dishes that the train staff sold and that passengers then placed on the small tables that separated the seats. It was more of a picnic than a trip, and two hours seemed too short. That was all it took to reach the town of Yiliang, where I waved goodbye to the Hanoi Express. Yiliang was still twenty kilometers short of the Stone Forest, and I thought I would have no trouble catching a bus. However, I soon learned there were no buses going there from Yiliang for another hour. Rather than wait, I walked out to the highway and flagged down the next bus passing by. Thirty minutes later, I arrived in Lunan and was looking forward to seeing Yunnan's most famous scenic wonder.

It was only 125 kilometers southeast of Kunming and was already becoming a major tourist destination. But its fame was not recent. Over 2,300 years ago, Ch'u Yuan, China's first great poet, asked, "Could there be a forest of stone?" A thousand years later, another poet answered, "Why not a forest of stone?" Were they just being cute, or had they heard about the rock formations outside the town of Lunan?

Either way, Yunnan's Stone Forest had been on the itinerary of Chinese travelers for at least three hundred years. Nowadays thousands of people visited every day. In terms of size, the main concentration covered an area of twelve square kilometers, or two hundred acres, which meant it was not too big to walk through in a few hours. Most tourists only came for the day and limited their exploration to the central part near the entrance, then headed back to Kunming.

Since I hoped to see more than the part near the entrance, I checked in at the hotel just outside the front gate then hired a guide to lead me through the maze and to tell me stories. My guide was a young Sani girl, and she was dressed in traditional Sani attire. The first thing she did after leading me into the forest of limestone pinnacles was to teach me how to use a leaf to make music. She reached into a bush and plucked a leaf the size and shape of a tea leaf. She said the thinner the leaf, the better. Camellia leaves, she said, were too thick. Then she held the leaf against her rose-red lower lip and blew. I watched with rapt attention, then I tried it. Or at least I tried to try it. The only sound I got was

Sani girl blowing on leaf

more of a sputter than anything resembling a musical note. Maybe I needed a thinner leaf, or maybe softer lips.

After that initial demonstration, she led me up a set of stairs to Lion Pavilion, where I had a grand view of the Stone Forest's massed gray waves of rock interspersed with the odd tree or tour group. According to her, the forest was created a long, long time ago, when the world was still a mysterious place and farmers were just learning their trade. Here in Sani country, one of the villagers hit on the idea of making a dam. His name was Chin-feng Lo-k'a. One night he snuck into the home of a powerful wizard and stole the magic whip the wizard used to move mountains. Then Chin-feng Lo-k'a snuck back outside, and all night long he used the whip to round up mountains and drive them like sheep toward the valley where he wanted to build his dam. But just before he had achieved his goal, he heard the crowing of the first cock. With the arrival of dawn, the whip lost its power, and the rocks and hills stopped moving. And when the wizard caught up with Chin-feng Lo-k'a, he split his skull and ate his brains, then sent him off to the Netherworld to join other unsuccessful heroes. Such was the origin of Stone Forest, and I looked down on it and marveled. I especially marveled at the gall of the calligrapher who left two huge Chinese characters in red paint on one of the rock pinnacles. They dominated the view, as if some artist had placed his seal right in the middle of a painting rather than along the margin. The two characters were the name Shih-lin, or Stone Forest, in Chinese. The graffiti was the work of Chu Te, the man who led the Red Army with the magic whip of Maoist thought until his troops heard the red rooster of capitalism.

After viewing Chu Te's graffiti, we walked back down to ground level and continued along a path until we came to a section of the gray lime-stone woods where a hundred tourists were taking turns getting dressed in traditional Sani clothes and having their picture taken in front of a pond with a rock formation in the background. According to my guide, the rock formation was the spirit of A-shih-ma. A-shih-ma, she said, was a Sani maiden who lived here a long time ago with her family, until one day a lecherous wizard carried her off to his castle. Before the wizard

Stone Forest

could force her to teach him how to make music with a leaf, A-shih-ma's brother, A-hei, rescued her, and they fled into the Stone Forest. But before they could reach the safety of their village, the wizard unleashed a terrible flood that raced through the limestone crags and swallowed A-shih-ma and her brother. Her spirit came to rest in this rock. And on the twenty-fourth day of the sixth lunar month, all the Sani come here to honor her spirit with a Torch Festival. The festival begins with horse racing and bullfighting and mud wrestling, then moves on to singing and dancing and drinking, and culminates with a torchlight parade through the limestone woods to the accompaniment of Sani banjos and drums and leaf-blowing boys and girls.

Since I wasn't interested in dressing up, I continued on through the maze of peaks. I think I must have seen a thousand of them. Finally, I told the Sani maiden who made sure I didn't get lost that I had seen enough, and we returned to the entrance. I was tired, and I headed for my room in the Stone Forest Hotel to rest up for the evening performance of singing and dancing put on by members of the Sani tribe. But first came dinner. I chose the duck. The specialty of the Lunan area involved taking your basic duck, rubbing its skin with sesame oil, and roasting it in a clay oven heated by a fire of pine needles. It was delicious, especially accompanied by some fried cheese, another Yunnan specialty. Once the duck and cheese were out of the way, it was time for the Stone Forest Karaoke across the road from my hotel. The show began around eight thirty and consisted of Sani boys playing high-pitched flutes and long-necked, loosely-tuned banjos, and girls playing their leaves. The duck was far more memorable.

鄭和

16. Cheng Ho

T HE NEXT MORNING, I returned to Kunming the customary way, by bus. But I only stayed long enough to deposit my bag at one of the city's bus stations and buy a ticket to my next destination. Kunming was at the north end of Tienchih Lake, and my next destination was at the south end. It was the hometown of one of the world's greatest sailors. His name was Cheng Ho, and he was the descendant of one of the Mongol generals who governed Yunnan during the Yuan dynasty.

Cheng Ho was born in 1371, shortly after the Chinese ended Mongol rule over the Middle Kingdom and established the Ming dynasty. Cheng Ho's family, though, remained loyal to the Mongol khan, as did other prominent families in this area, and it took ten years for the Chinese to regain control of the province. When they did, they killed those who had put up resistance. Because he was only ten, Cheng Ho's life was spared, but he was castrated to prevent him from fathering Mongol-sympathetic descendents. He was then forced to serve in the army and was later sent to serve as a eunuch at court, where he distinguished himself for his diplomacy. In fact, he became such a favorite of the emperor, the emperor sent him on one of the world's greatest diplomatic missions.

In 1405 Cheng Ho sailed from the east coast of China to the Indian Ocean. His voyage, like Columbus's, was spurred, in part, by interest in trade but also reflected the dynasty's desire to expand its influence, much as the Mongols had done during the previous dynasty in Central Asia. But the Chinese emperor had diplomacy, not conquest, in mind.

To make sure everyone Cheng Ho met would understand what sort of potentate they were dealing with, the emperor provided his Mongol admiral with the largest fleet ever assembled in the ancient world. I headed for Cheng Ho's hometown on one of the buses that left Kunming every hour, and ninety minutes later got off in the town of Kunyang. The Cheng Ho Memorial was on a hill a kilometer away overlooking the south end of Tienchih Lake.

When Cheng Ho sailed from the east coast of China, his fleet included sixty-two of the biggest ships ever built and over one hundred smaller vessels. Most of the big ships were built at the Lungchiang boatyard near Nanking. As amazing as it might sound, they were 120 meters long and 50 meters abeam and weighed a thousand tons. They carried nine masts and crews that ranged from four hundred to a thousand men. Each of these ships was ten times the size of those sailed by Columbus eighty-seven years later. And while the *Niña*, the *Pinta*, and the *Santa María* carried fewer than a hundred men, Cheng Ho's fleet carried an army of twenty-eight thousand in addition to the crews.

It must have been an awesome spectacle to see them sail into the harbors of the small kingdoms that dotted the South Asian trade routes. The mind reels trying to imagine the logistics involved. But despite the size of his fleet, Cheng Ho sailed successfully around the tip of India and all the way to the Red Sea and the east coast of Africa. And over the space of twenty-eight years, he made the trip seven times. On one such voyage, he brought back emissaries from over thirty kingdoms, and on his next voyage, he took them back home. It was a thirty-thousand-kilometer round-trip aided by little more than compass and astrolabe. The only detailed maps were those in the sky. But the wine-dark sea was kind to Cheng Ho. Doubtlessly, the sea gods were also impressed with his diplomacy.

Who would have guessed that on the shores of an inland lake, about as far from the sea as you can get in China, one of the world's greatest sailors was born? I expected that the Cheng Ho Memorial Hall would have celebrated such a hometown hero. But all the memorial hall had to show for its native son were a few photos of the family's current generation of descendants and the odd piece of flotsam from what must have been a very rich cargo. Other than the caretaker, no one else was there.

On my way back down the hill, I paused at Cheng Ho's father's grave. Cheng Ho's own grave was in Nanking, not far from the former site of the Lungchiang boatyard. The trick, according to Cheng Ho, was to catch the northeasterly wind in late fall and to ride that wind all the way to India, then to catch the southwesterly wind in spring, and to ride that wind all the way back to China. It wasn't as easy as he made it sound. In his own case, he usually arrived in India after the southwesterly wind had begun to blow and ended up spending a year waiting for a chance to go home the following spring. He caught his last southwesterly in the Persian Gulf in 1433 and rode it all the way back to Nanking. And he is still there, under a grass-covered mound, waiting for another northeasterly to take him back to Mecca again. Like his father, Cheng Ho was a Muslim. For all his great achievements, he was simply a humble pilgrim.

西雙版納

17. Hsishuangbanna

AFTER RETRIEVING MY BAG at the Kunming bus station, I took another bus to the airport. The first day I arrived in Kunming I bought a plane ticket to Hsishuangbanna, four hundred kilometers south of Kunming. Now it was time to use it. Hsishuangbanna. The name was so smooth in the mouth, it reminded me of one of Trader Vic's rum and fruit juice concoctions, the kind served in a coconut shell with a paper parasol and a couple of long straws. I could have used a Hsishuangbanna before I boarded my plane. It was the end of my first hot day in Yunnan. But the only thing they had at the airport with alcohol was a warm wine cooler. They didn't even have ice cubes. Hsishuangbanna. I said it again, but it didn't make my wine cooler any cooler. I left the bottle on the table half-full and boarded my plane. Forty-five minutes later, I was there, in Hsishuangbanna. The airport was new and was built in imitation of a Tai-style house—except it wasn't on stilts. The Tai were the largest ethnic minority in Hsishuangbanna, and I would be meeting them soon enough, but the first person to greet me was Merle Haggard singing on the airport loudspeaker about heartbreak in Mississippi. But I wasn't in Mississippi. I was in Hsishuangbanna, where the girls walk down the streets carrying paper parasols. It was the first thing I noticed as my taxi whisked me from the airport to the southeast edge of town.

I passed up the usual hotel scene and rented a room instead in an old Tai-style house. Half the second floor was an inn, and the other half was

Restaurant mural in Hsishuangbanna

a restaurant. And the restaurant included an outside veranda where I sat down and ordered black rice and fried river moss and a cold beer. The gods were smiling and so was I.

I was in Hsishuangbanna. In the local Tai language, "hsishuang-banna" means "twelve districts." The name was given to this twenty-thousand square kilometer region along China's border with Burma and Laos in the sixteenth century, three hundred years after the Mongols first brought it under Chinese control. The capital of Hsishuangbanna is Chinghung, where I was sitting on the veranda glad to be there and not on the road. The plane took forty-five minutes to fly four hundred kilometers and only cost 200RMB, or 40 bucks. The alternative would have been to take the bus. But the bus took two days to cover a zigzag distance of seven hundred kilometers. The savings wasn't that much compared to the loss of time and sleep and possibly hearing if you sat near the driver. To make sure I wouldn't have to endure the bus going back, the first thing I did at the airport after arriving in Chinghung was to make a reservation on a flight back to Kunming.

The veranda was sweet, as was Chinghung. But I wasn't on vacation, and the next morning I caught one of the hourly buses heading north. I wanted to visit Hsishuangbanna's wild elephant reserve. And less than two hours after leaving Chinghung, that was where I got off. There was a sign on the side of the road announcing the Sancha River Butterfly Farm but no mention of elephants. I was somewhat puzzled, but the driver insisted that this was the place. Right next to the sign was a small restaurant, so I walked inside to ask directions. I was in luck. Sitting at one of the tables was one of the reserve's guides. After I told him what I wanted to do, he led me down the slope to a set of buildings that housed the administrative offices of the butterfly farm and the elephant reserve and also some exhibits. He showed me 168 kinds of butterflies, including one that looked like a pair of leaves. There was also a huge aviary where they bred butterflies, but it was March, and the caterpillars were still dreaming.

After showing me the aviary, my guide led me into the forest. First we both ducked under the electric wire they turned on at night to keep the

Elephant reserve hotel

elephants on the other side. The reserve included an area of ten thousand hectares and was home to 140 wild elephants, 18 of which could usually be found in the area encompassed by a system of trails within a few kilometers of the reserve headquarters. And oops, what was that I almost stepped in? It was a five-pound pile of elephant poop. And it was fresh. My guide looked at the poop, which consisted mostly of straw. Then he looked along the trail and pointed to a swath of tall grass that wasn't tall anymore. It looked like someone had dragged a log through it. He said an elephant must have walked through the day before, or perhaps the night before. The elephants were usually active at night, he said, preferring to sleep in the forest during the day. They were Asian elephants and had an average weight of between three and four tons. And they were dangerous. My guide said the director of the reserve had narrowly escaped being killed on three separate occasions. And visitors were warned to keep their voices down.

At one point my guide told me not to move, then disappeared to investigate something he had heard in the bushes. When he reappeared, he said it was just a wild pig. He said there were also wild oxen in the reserve as well as monkeys, lorises, deer, and at last count sixty-two kinds of birds, including white-tailed pheasants. After nearly two hours of wandering through the jungle and across rickety bamboo bridges, we reached an open area where a fairly large stream formed a series of pools. There were two huts on either side of the stream—but the huts weren't on the ground. One was in a banyan tree directly above one of the pools, and another larger hut was further away on ten-meter-high stilts. They made up the nature reserve "hotel," complete with bunks and sleeping bags and mosquito nets. My guide said around midnight the elephants came to drink and bathe, and people who stayed there overnight usually didn't get any sleep. He said if the moon was out, it was an amazing sight. And if it was dark, you could creep down to the edge of the river for a closer look, assuming your heart was up for a little adrenalin.

My guide said I could see more of the reserve by taking what he called the Danger Trail, but he also said the authorities insisted that anyone who did so be accompanied by five armed guides. Meeting a wild bull elephant on the trail was a distinct possibility and not a very pleasant experience. Fortunately, elephants have a hard time climbing, and the trick, he said, is to scramble up the nearest hill before the elephant can grab you with its trunk or step on your head. Naturally, there used to be a lot more wild elephants in this part of China, but I was surprised there were still any at all, especially after seeing what happened to wildlife at the beginning of my trip in Wuchou. Since I didn't have the time or the adrenalin for the Danger Trail, I asked my guide to lead me back to where I got off the bus. I wanted to visit another reserve, but one that was safer. He waited on the roadside with me and helped me wave down the next bus heading back to Chinghung.

勐侖

18. Menglun

AFTER ANOTHER DINNER of black rice and river moss on the veranda and yet another cold beer—I figured I was soon going to be beyond its reach. I said goodbye to such delights and caught a bus early the next morning to the town of Menglun, which was eighty kilometers southeast of Chinghung. Menglun is the site of China's one and only tropical plant research center, where you sleep with orchids instead of elephants. The thought was appealing. Whenever I thought of the tropics, I thought of a jungle, and I was looking forward to disappearing into a dark landscape shaded from the sun by huge trees and hanging vines. As the bus I was on followed the Lantsang, or Mekong, south from Chinghung, it was evident from the amount of mud in the river and along its banks that my image of the tropics would need some readjusting. My image would have to include massive deforestation. When I first landed at the airport, I was surprised at how green everything looked from the air, and I imagined I was entering a region of endless tropical forests. But at ground level the illusion soon gave way to the reality of endless rubber tree plantations.

Over the previous three decades, Hsishuangbanna had become a major center for rubber production in China, second only to Hainan Island. That was what happened after the Tropical Crops Research Institute in Chinghung introduced new and better kinds of rubber trees. The new trees grew faster and produced more rubber than earlier varieties. Rubber had now outstripped tea, sugar cane, and rice as the region's biggest cash crop. Meanwhile, the region's tropical forests had become about as rare as wild elephants.

The bus I was on followed the muddy Mekong as far as the town of Menghan, where it finally left that saddest of rivers and turned east. An hour later, I was walking down the one-street town of Menglun. A minute later, or maybe two, I had paid an entry fee and was walking on the suspension bridge at the end of town that led across the Losuo River to the Tropical Plant Research Center. I wasn't the first foreigner to cross that bridge. A casual glance at the research center's brochure I received with my entry ticket revealed that I was following in the footsteps of HRH, the Duck of Edinburgh. I always knew Prince Philip had an affinity for animals. He was, after all, president of the World Wildlife Federation. But who would have guessed he was related to mallards and pintails? While I chuckled at the misprint in the brochure, halfway across the suspension bridge, I stopped to watch two boys using an air gun to shoot fish in the river. They didn't seem to be having much luck, and I wondered why they weren't using dynamite. Nothing like a couple sticks of TNT to get a fish's attention.

I continued across the bridge to Gourd Island. In 1959, Chinese botanist Ts'ai Hsi-t'ao came here with a handful of assistants and set up a research center to study tropical plants. Since then, the center's staff had grown to include more than 400 workers, 150 of whom held advanced degrees in botany, organic chemistry, and medicine. Near the center's offices, I stopped at a marker erected in Professor Ts'ai's memory. Beside it was a fine specimen of what the Chinese called the dragon-blood tree. As early as the T'ang dynasty, Chinese doctors were using a powder made from the tree's resin to stop bleeding and at the same time to stimulate circulation and tissue growth. In the intervening centuries, however, knowledge of the tree's existence was lost, until Professor Ts'ai rediscovered it on a nearby mountain.

According to the brochure, the Tropical Plant Research Center occupied an area of nine hundred hectares along the Losuo River, and most of the grounds were open to the public, including a large hothouse devoted to orchids. Since the center was first established in 1959, more

A tree in the Tropical Plant Research Center

than three thousand tropical plants from all over the world had been grown here for the purpose of research, including several species that had aroused the interest of cancer researchers around the world.

Near the administrative offices, there was a hostel and also a guide service for visitors who wanted to do more than stroll through the bamboo and banyans. While I was still doing just that, I paused to buy a few red, heart-shaped seeds from a Tai woman. The Chinese call them "hsiang-ssu-tou," which means "miss-you seeds." These seeds have been associated with love for more than a thousand years. They definitely have magic powers, and a word of warning is in order. They got me into trouble once when I gave a necklace of them to a girl who admired them. A few days later, she knocked on my door with a red rose in her hand and romance in her eyes, and I had a hard time convincing her the necklace was an innocent gift. This time I put the seeds in my pocket, figuring I would only take them out in case of emergency.

As I continued through the park-like forest, I met a young Han Chinese who made his living teaching English and leading the occasional group of foreigners to the more primitive villages in the area. That sounded like a good idea, and I hired him to do exactly that. He didn't waste any time. He went into the research center's office and told them he would be gone for a few days, and we started off along a trail that led north to the Tai village of Chengtzu and the home of the people of the golden teeth.

A half dozen ethnic groups live in Hsishuangbanna, including the Pulang, the Lahu, the Chinuo, the Wa, and the Yao, but the two largest groups are the Aini and the Tai, both with more than a million members inside China and several million more scattered through the northern parts of Burma, Laos, and Thailand. The village of Chengtzu had more than a thousand residents, making it one of the largest Tai villages in the region. Like all Tai villages, it consisted of wooden houses built on stilts with the living quarters on the second floor and room for pigs and farm tools and the family latrine on the first. The Tai are rice growers, and it is rare to find a Tai village very far from a plain or a well-watered valley. Some scientists think that the ancestors of the Tai were the ones

Tai village of Chengtzu

who first introduced rice to the tribes to the north, including those living along the Yangtze. If true, that would push the prehistory of the Tai back as far as that of the Han Chinese—to more than seven thousand years ago.

The Tai, though, didn't come to the attention of the Chinese until 2,100 years ago, when Ssu-ma Ch'ien called this region "the land of elephant riders." No one knows how long the Tai had been living here before that, but they have been living here ever since. And over the centuries they have been called by many names besides "elephant riders," including "people of the white clothes" and "people of the golden teeth." When I visited, they still wore white shirts, and they still capped their teeth with gold, but they didn't ride elephants anymore. If they rode anything, it was a bicycle.

Chengtzu was about five kilometers from the Tropical Plant Research Center, and the reason my guide led me there was that several of his former students lived in Chengtzu. He stopped at the gate of one house and yelled, and a boy came out onto the veranda and invited us up. The gate was little more than a few sticks of wood lashed together with vines, and my guide pushed it open. I followed him up the wooden stairs that led to the veranda, and we entered the cool shade of the house's interior. The family was just sitting down to lunch, and we joined them. It was fairly simple: rice, vegetables, and a dish of pork fat. Afterwards, we all stretched out on the long benches built into the sides of the open-air living area. Even though it was mid-March, I was in the tropics, where it didn't pay to do anything after lunch except sleep.

As soon as the shadows got long enough, my guide and I got up, and he led me to the village's Buddhist temple. Along with the Tibetans, the Tai have to be the most Buddhist ethnic group in China. But unlike the Tibetans, who follow the Tantric, Vajrayana form of Buddhism, the Tai follow the more ancient, conservative form known as Theravada, which is the tradition followed by most Buddhists throughout Southeast Asia.

Compared to other Buddhist temples in China, Tai temples are simple affairs. This one was located on a grassy knoll at the edge of the village, and it included a sixteenth-century pagoda that held the remains of

Buddhist temple at Chengtzu

monks of the past and a large wooden shrine hall. There were no other structures, except for a wooden fence that surrounded the knoll. A sign at the door asked us to remove our shoes, and the cement floor felt cool as I bowed down to pay my respects before the hall's small altar. A dozen woven tapestries depicting events in the Buddha's life hung from the roof. They twisted lightly in the breeze, and half a dozen candles sputtered on the altar.

It was early afternoon, and the older monks were still asleep on mat-covered benches in a shady area at the rear of the hall. Since there was no one to talk to, we put our shoes back on and headed out the rear gate. Just beyond the gate, a dozen young monks were busy tamping gunpowder into bamboo tubes. I was puzzled and asked them what the gunpowder was for. They couldn't speak Mandarin, only Tai, and my guide had to translate. It turned out the biggest local Buddhist festival of the year was only days away, and they were making rockets for the Buddha. The oldest among them couldn't have been more than twelve. Like the older monks, who were still dreaming monk dreams, they kept their heads more or less shaved, they wore their yellow robes over one shoulder, and they were barefoot. But they were still children. And the game that day was making skyrockets for the big festival, after which it would be back to the books. Most Tai families send their sons to the temples to become monks for a few years because that's where they learn to read and write the Tai script that has been in use for the past two thousand years. They also learn how to make a decent rocket.

Since blast-off was still a few days away, we said goodbye and headed down the knoll to the edge of a forest, where a group of Tai women were standing around a bunch of wooden posts. On closer inspection, the posts turned out to be the sawed-off trunks of rubber trees, and one of the women was showing the others how to cut a trunk on the side with a long-handled gouge at a thirty-degree angle in order to draw out as much sap as possible without injuring the tree. I stopped to watch, but it wasn't as interesting as making rockets, and we continued on.

From Chengtzu, my guide led me along the Losuo River, and after several kilometers through another Tai village. The village was Man-an, and my guide stopped long enough to make arrangements with the family of another of his former students for us to spend the night. Once that was taken care of, we headed up a mountain on a dirt trail that had been made by the rain as much as by foot traffic. An hour later, we arrived at the Aini village of Taka.

The Tai and the Aini are the major ethnic groups in Hsishuangbanna, but they occupy different ecological niches. The Tai occupy the plains and the valley bottoms, and the Aini occupy the slopes. The Chinese refer to the Aini as Hani, but in Hsishuangbanna they refer to themselves as Aini. In the Aini language, "ai" means "animal" and "ni" means "people." According to Aini legends, the ancestors of the animal people lived in the plains much further east, and they migrated to the mountains between the Mekong and the Red River at least 2,200 years ago, which was when they were first noticed by Chinese historians.

In the intervening centuries, their lives hadn't changed much, and entering the village of Taka was like stepping back a thousand years. Unlike the Tai, the Aini usually live beyond the reach of power lines. As we arrived, we stumbled around the village with our flashlights. After making a few inquiries, we found a house where half the village had gathered for a wedding feast and a night of hard drinking. We were just in time. Wedding festivities usually last three nights, and we arrived on the second night, when the groom's family invited all their relatives and the bride's relatives for a big feast.

There must have been a hundred people in the house either cooking or serving food or sitting around short bamboo tables on equally short wooden stools. Instead of plates, everyone was eating off banana leaves and drinking out of bamboo cups. Mostly they were eating pig. The family had butchered a pig just before we arrived, and in less than an hour it was on the table in half a dozen forms. One such form was pig's liver, and it was incredible. It was like eating a fine steak. A finer piece of liver I had never eaten. I don't know if that was because it was so fresh or because mountain pigs simply ate better. Another delicious and unusual dish was homemade tofu pudding. The unusual part was the bamboo ladle with which we ate it. The bowl of the ladle was made from a bamboo tube about two inches across, and the handle was simply the stem of a branch that was left on the bamboo.

We ate and ate and lost track of what we ate because we also drained a bathtub of rice wine. All I recall was toasting the bride and groom and waving goodbye under a big tangerine moon as we staggered back down the mountain along a trail of fireflies to Man-an. Man-an had electricity, and the members of the Tai family we had arranged to stay with were gathered around their new TV set watching a Taiwan soap opera. By the time the father came home, we were asleep on the floor.

According to my guide, visitors could almost always find a place to sleep in a Tai village, but the same was not true of Aini villages. It was not so much that the Aini were less hospitable but that the Aini were mountain people, whereas the Tai were flatlanders and more accustomed to dealing with strangers. The Tai also had more to offer in the way of material comforts, and I was grateful for the luxury of a cotton blanket and a cotton-filled mattress pad, both of which were a lot cleaner than me.

Aini village of New Motung

The next morning, our hosts served up hot rice gruel and leftovers from their dinner the night before. I was still feeling the effects of the wedding banquet, and the food helped. So did getting back on the trail. It made me think of something other than my head. From Man-an, we spent two hours retracing the dirt trail that led back to the Tropical Plant Research Center on Gourd Island. According to the center's brochure, the island is actually a peninsula shaped like a gourd. At the wedding banquet the previous night, an Aini woman told me the real reason why it's called Gourd Island. According to her, the Aini believe that all the world's creatures and plants came from seeds contained in a magic gourd.

But we didn't stop to see the three thousand descendents of those seeds the center had collected. We walked through the center's grounds and re-crossed the suspension bridge that led back to the town of Menglun and took the next bus headed back toward the regional capital of Chinghung. Twenty kilometers later, we got off at the Aini village of Motung, crossed the road, and started up a trail that led to another Aini village of the same name. An hour up the trail, we passed an Aini woman carrying a bundle on her head and sortly after that an Aini

Aini woman on the trail

hunter. He was carrying an ancient flintlock rifle, and he gave us a sample of his female pheasant call. A few minutes later, just as we crossed the ridge, I heard the high-pitched answer of a male. If we were lucky, I thought, we would be eating pheasant that night. I didn't hear a shot, though, and resigned myself to more pig for dinner.

After another hour, just before we reached New Motung, we met an old man on the trail. He was carrying the trunk of a banana tree. The banana tree, he said, was for his pigs, and he invited us to his house for dinner. The old man said that since the road had been paved in Old Motung, there were too many people living there, so he had moved with his sons and nephews thirteen years earlier and started a new village higher up. There were about a dozen wooden houses in the village, and he led us up the stairs into the second floor of his.

The village was located at the edge of a ridge, and as the sun went down, I sat on the veranda and watched the lights of Old Motung start to flicker far below like stars at the bottom of a sea. The villagers had channeled water to their village from a small reservoir by means of bamboo pipes, and one of the pipes led to a makeshift shower, where the village boys were washing off before dinner. I wasn't sure where the girls took their showers, but I was surprised at the lack of concern shown by Aini women in exposing their breasts or private parts, which became evident whenever we sat down on the floor.

As the sun finally set on New Motung, my hosts yelled for me to come inside for some new rice wine and a plate of bauhinia flowers. I was soon practicing the only Aini word I needed to know: "chi-ba-t'ou," which means "bottoms up." It was mid-March, and everywhere in Hsishuangbanna the hillsides were covered with bauhinia trees in bloom. The bauhinia is the official flower of Hong Kong. It's even on their money. In Aini country it's a vegetable, and a delicious one at that. They take the middle part of the flower and blanch it in boiling water for a few seconds, then fry it in oil with a little pepper and a dash of vinegar. It was just the thing to accompany a new batch of rice wine.

Like most rice wine, this was made from glutinous rice, but my host said that he steeped his in twenty-seven different wild plants for at least a month. It had a kick, and it was only a month old, but it was as smooth as good whiskey. Once we had been sufficiently kicked in the head, his wife brought out the main courses, including steamed, home-grown rice, fried peanuts, and cabbage with chunks of pork fat, all of which were served on banana leaves.

While we were eating, my host explained the Aini naming system. Each of his children had a two-syllable name, the first syllable of which was the last syllable of his own name. The Aini don't use family names, only what amounts to generational and personal names. The system has an immense advantage in tracing ancestry. My host said he could trace his own back fifty-four generations, back to a man named Chuo-miu, who moved to that region 1,600 years ago. Before that, there was A-ka La-yu, whose first child was the ancestor of the Wa, whose second child was the ancestor of the Aini, whose third child was the ancestor of the Tai, whose fourth child was the ancestor of the Han Chinese, and whose fifth child, born at midnight, was the ancestor of the spirit world.

The next morning I woke up in what felt like an in-between world and was glad that I remembered to bring along some instant coffee. I was in serious need of it. After pouring hot water from one of the family's half dozen thermoses into the magic powder, I sat down outside on the veranda and watched the morning sun burn off the mist that hung in the surrounding valleys. While I was still waiting for my coffee to cool off, a group of Aka came through the village. They were a hunting party. According to my host, there were still tigers and bears in the area.

He also said that there were still a few wild elephants out there that everyone avoided. He laughed and recounted how one day his ten-year-old son met a wild elephant and couldn't find a hill to run up, so he climbed a big banyan tree. The elephant was so mad when it found out it couldn't knock down the banyan, it stayed at the bottom of the tree for three days waiting for the boy to come down. But the boy was no fool, and he stayed put. As the days and nights wore on, the boy cried for help, but he was too far from his village. Finally, on the fourth day, a village search party found him and managed to chase the elephant away by setting fire to the surrounding grass—their flintlocks were useless against the big brute's thick hide. My host laughed about how his son almost starved to death, and his son grinned too.

The Aka hunting party, meanwhile, passed through on their way back to their own village—apparently, empty-handed. After watching them disappear over the adjacent ridge, I finished my coffee and suggested to my guide that we follow them. He said their village was about two hours away along one of the trails that led back to the main road. And that was where we headed.

The Aka are another branch of the Aini, and thereon hangs a tale, or, more accurately, a tail. It seems that a long time ago when the Aini were just one of the many animals of the forest, the chief of the tribe sighed that if only they could learn how to grow rice, they wouldn't have to live like their brothers, Tiger and Monkey. Rice seeds, though, were the property of the gods. Still, the chief promised that whoever could steal the rice seeds from the gods could marry his daughter, and she was such a lovely creature that all the men in the village vied with one another to steal the seeds. But the gods were alert to their tricks, and none of the village men succeeded. The village dog, though, also overheard the chief's promise, and one night it snuck into the house of the gods and stole the rice seeds and brought them back to the village. As was the case with the Yao, the chief kept his promise and married his loveliest of daughters to the village dog, and the Aka are descendants of that union.

In the Aini language, "aka" means "dog," and the dog people still honor their ancestral hero by refusing to eat dog meat, at least inside their houses. Once a year, though, every Aka village kills at least one dog and hangs its body at the village gate as an offering to the gods for stealing their rice seeds.

As we followed the trail to one of their villages, I couldn't help noticing that most of the hillsides along the way were missing their trees. The Aini, and their cousins the Aka, still used the old slash-and-burn technique for clearing mountain slopes to create fields, and they had cleared everything within walking distance of their village. According to my guide, the Aini and Aka use a field for three years, then let it rest for another three before using it again. Their main crop is rice, but it's dry rice, which depends on the summer rainy season instead of irrigation for water. Along the way we also passed the occasional forest that contained the odd sacred spring, which was the only thing that saved it from being cleared for another rice field. Despite their slash-and-burn farming, at least the Aini understood that you don't mess with your water source—a rule modern man still has trouble learning to follow. My friend Gary Snyder once told me that the two most important questions friends of the earth should ask themselves are, Where does my water come from? and Where does my garbage go? The Aini knew where their water came from. They also knew where their garbage went. It went to feed their pigs. Plastic was so new to them, they refused to throw away a comb that had lost most of its teeth and instead stuck it over their doorway just in case it might come in handy again. They also put the few glass bottles that came into their possession on their roof to ensure their family had a never-ending source of blessings.

After two hours, we finally reached the Aka village where the hunters were from, and we paused long enough for a drink of water and to exchange mountain gossip—at least my guide exchanged gossip. I just sat there on a bench thinking about the water. I recalled the Chinese saying: "When you drink the water, think of the source." I also remembered that I hadn't had a bath in three days.

基諾族

19. The Chinuo

A N HOUR LATER, we were back on the paved road. I thanked my guide for such a memorable few days and crossed his palm with the equivalent of 50 bucks for his help. I waited for a bus heading back to Chinghung and finally caught a ride on a tour bus. It was heading back to Chinghung, but it was going the long way. About halfway, it stopped to let passengers stroll through a Chinuo village a few hundred meters from the road. It was a strange experience, and one that I wouldn't want to repeat. The Chinuo are one of China's smallest ethnic groups as well as one of its more primitive. They weren't even recognized as an ethnic group until 1979. At last count there were eighteen thousand Chinuo living in China, all of them in forty or so villages in the mountains north of Menglun. The Chinuo call this area "the place the Chinese couldn't find." Obviously, they're going to have to change the name. In any case, they weren't at all happy to have a dozen Chinese tourists and a foreigner walking through their village. As we approached, the doors of the village long house closed, and the Chinuo stayed inside until we were gone. But that didn't mean I didn't hear any Chinuo stories.

While no one knows how long the Chinuo have been living in Hsishuangbanna, if you ask the Chinuo, they'll tell you they have been there since the great flood. Yes, the great flood. It would be hard to find a people anywhere on the planet without a memory of that event, and the Chinuo are no exception. Here is their version of the story, which I read in a book I bought in Chinghung: a long, long time ago, not long after the world was created and life began, the waters of the world's oceans began to rise, and people began to drown, and the parents of Ma-hei and Ma-niu decided they had to do something to save their son and daughter. They hit on the idea of making a huge drum, and the father went into the forest to cut down a tree. But as soon as his axe cut into the tree's bark, the tree cried out in pain. This was back when people could still communicate with other life forms. It was also when people still respected other life forms. When the father tried another tree, the same thing happened. And it happened ninety-nine times, until the father finally gave up and returned to his house.

Now it was his wife's turn, and she went out into their yard and bowed down in front of a huge loquat tree. The tree had supplied them with its fruit for many years, and now the wife asked it for its wood. The tree wanted to help the family out, but to help would mean its own demise. What to do? Well, the loquat tree was a truly kindhearted tree, and it agreed. The father and mother then cut it down and made a huge drum. They then put their two children inside along with a little rooster and some food and kissed them goodbye as the floodwaters swept them away—the parents to a watery grave, and their children, Ma-hei and Ma-niu, to the wide-open sea. And the sea was all the children saw for nine days and nine nights, until finally the little rooster crowed, and Ma-hei and Ma-niu woke up and discovered that their drum had come to ground on a mountain. They got out, and as the waters receded, they started to explore the adjacent valleys. But except for an old tree, there was nothing: no plants, no animals, and no people. Fortunately, they still had a single gourd seed left over from their provisions. They planted it, and it soon covered the mountain with its vines and gourds, which they lived off of. The days went by, and so did the years, and the handsome Ma-hei and lovely Ma-niu grew old.

Finally Ma-hei said to Ma-niu: "Ma-niu, we're the only people left. If we don't have children, the human race will die out." But Ma-niu said, "How can we do that? Brothers and sisters can't have children." Ma-hei scratched his head, then suggested, "Why don't you ask the old tree in the forest if we can have children?" Well, Ma-niu couldn't think of anything better, so she walked into the forest to ask the old tree. But while she was pushing her way through all the vines that covered the ground, her brother took a shortcut and reached the tree first and hid behind it. When Ma-niu arrived and asked the old tree what to do, Ma-hei made a voice like a tree and said, "What else can you do? Go back and multiply." So Ma-niu went back, and told Ma-hei what the tree had said. Ma-hei acted sufficiently surprised as well as more than a little pleased, and he led his sister into their hut to multiply. But it was no use. They were simply too old.

And so Ma-hei and Ma-niu resigned themselves to being the world's last humans. As they grew older, they devoted what little energy they had to collecting enough gourds to eat. Then, one day, they brought back an especially large gourd, and Ma-hei started to cut into the gourd with his knife. Suddenly a voice from inside the gourd cried out, "No, don't cut there. I'll die." Ma-hei lived in the old days when spirits were everywhere, even in gourds. He turned the gourd over and tried another spot, and another voice cried out, "No, don't cut there. I'll die." Well, this happened several more times, until finally the voice of an old woman cried out, "Cut here. My name is A-p'i K'ao-k'ao. I'm old. It's okay if I die, as long as my children survive." And so Ma-hei cut into the spot where the voice had come from and made a hole in the gourd. And out of the hole came four humans. The first was the ancestor of the Pulang people. The second was the ancestor of the Han Chinese. The third was the ancestor of the Tai people. And the fourth and last to come out was the ancestor of the Chinuo people, whose story this was. In fact, "chinuo" means "last to come out." And to this day, the Chinuo still honor the old woman in the gourd from whom they are all descended. Before every banquet or festival, they set aside a bowl of rice and invite A-p'i K'ao-k'ao to join them. That's the story of the great flood, and any Chinuo will tell you that was the way it happened, assuming they open their doors for you.

勐龍

20. Menglung

B ACK IN CHINGHUNG, I reacquainted myself with the luxury of a hot
bath, then returned to my spot on the hotel veranda and planned my
next foray. I had already visited the areas north and east of Chinghung.
It was time to explore the area to the south, and the next morning I
boarded a bus headed in that direction. Unlike the more mountainous
areas to the north and east, the area to the south consisted of a series
of broad plains planted with rice and sugar cane between hills that had
been stripped of their original vegetation and replanted with rubber
trees. Along the way, we passed through a dozen Tai villages and even
a few one-street towns. Finally, after two hours, the bus reached the
end of the line: the town of Menglung, also known as Tamenglung, or
Greater Menglung.

Menglung was only eight kilometers from the Burma border. The
local Tai and Aini people were allowed to cross with little regard for
border formalities, but for foreigners and Han Chinese alike, Menglung
was the end of the line. The reason I wanted to visit Menglung was
to see what was left of its pagodas—which wasn't much. The Tai are
Buddhists, and their pagodas simple affairs—or they had become simple
affairs. The pagodas were all destroyed during the Cultural Revolution,
and those that had been rebuilt were made of cement, inlaid with mirror
chips, and painted with bright primary colors. Even in their primitive
form, though, they were a refreshing change from the more sedate brick
towers I had seen elsewhere in China.

Menglung's White Pagoda

Entrance to White Pagoda

After viewing a few of the smaller pagodas at the edge of the small town, I proceeded to Menglung's Black Pagoda. It was on a hill at the south edge of town. But it was no longer black. It was a faded white, and despite being the tallest pagoda in the region at twenty-seven meters, it wasn't an especially memorable piece of work. More mirror chips would have helped, I suppose. About the only thing of interest was the low surrounding wall, which was built to resemble a dragon whose undulating body set off the site as holy ground.

After seeing the sights of Menglung, such as they were, I started walking down the road that led back toward Chinghung to visit one last pagoda. After two kilometers, I came to the Tai village of Manfeilung. Most of the towns and villages in that region had a "meng" or a "man" at the beginning of their name. In the Tai language, "meng" refers to a town or group of villages, and "man" refers to a single village. From Manfeilung, or Flying Dragon Village, I followed a dirt path that led up the hill behind it. On my way, I stopped at a large Buddhist temple where several dozen monks were residing. But none of them could speak Mandarin, so I continued up the trail to the pagoda on top.

It was Hsishuangbanna's most famous pagoda, and it was known far and wide as the White Pagoda. It was first built in 1204, and it had been rebuilt many times since then. It looked like the last time hadn't been very long ago. As with the Black Pagoda, the main ingredients were cement and white paint, with yellow and red trim. There was also a shrine hall, but pilgrims did their bowing outside at the base of the pagoda. On closer inspection, I discovered why. The pagoda was built on a huge boulder, and when I walked over to the southwest corner of the boulder, I noticed a small niche at the base. The niche was covered with glass, and there was a slot for people to insert donations. I looked inside and saw the reason for their veneration. It was the Buddha's footprints. Yes, the Buddha's footprints. By some mysterious power the Buddha had traveled here from India and left his footprints on the surface of the boulder. Buddhist pilgrims came here from all over China, as well as from Burma and Laos and Thailand, to pay homage to the footprints, which, according to a sign, the Buddha left when he visited that part of the world at the age of sixty-two.

According to historical records, the pagoda itself wasn't erected until 1,700 years after the Buddha's visit. It wasn't surprising, though, to see footprints at a Theravadin Buddhist shrine. When Buddhism first developed as an organized religion, there were no statues of the Buddha, because it was felt that the human form somehow misrepresented the Buddha's message of liberation from all form. Instead, his disciples used his footprints to represent his transcendence from this world of dust. A pair of footprints was the only thing in the way of symbolism that early Buddhist shrines contained. I joined half a dozen other pilgrims in paying my respects before the niche, while a hundred flags flapped their prayers above us.

On my way out, a Tai woman who was helping take care of the pagoda told me that a big Buddhist festival would be taking place a few hours later nearby there. Suddenly I recalled my meeting a few days earlier with the young monks who were tamping gunpowder into bamboo tubes to make rockets. I was just in time for blast-off. The Buddhist festival was being held in the village of Manpo, and the woman gave me directions, which I followed by walking back down the hill to the road that connected Menglung with Chinghung, then north three kilometers to the village of Manlungkou, and finally east on a newly built road that led across a plain of rice fields.

It was still early afternoon, and this was supposed to be a lunar festival celebrated on the second full moon of the year, but the celebration was not waiting for the moon. The village of Manpo was about a kilometer from the main road, but I could hear the music long before I arrived. Several thousand villagers were already in the large grassy area beyond the village temple, and more were streaming in behind me.

As I arrived, I passed a row of local women selling various kinds of cooked food, much of it deep-fried or made of sticky, glutinous rice, and I stopped to sample my share. Then, beyond their makeshift stalls, I joined the crowd that had gathered around two groups of dancers. Each

Tai women watching the celebration

Tai skirts

Sky rockets for the Buddha

group had formed a circle of couples, with the girls on the inside and the boys on the outside. One of the circles was for married couples, and the other was for the single set. In the middle of each circle was a group of musicians beating on drums and gongs and cymbals. The circles of clumsy men and graceful women moved slowly around the musicians, three steps forward then a shuffle backward, with their hands describing the flight of swallows in the air.

In addition to the dancing and the music, every once in a while a skyrocket shot off from the launch-pad scaffolding of bamboo erected at the edge of the dance area. The villagers had a stack of rockets numbering well over a hundred. The basic design was to tie bamboo sections filled with gunpowder around a much longer cane of bamboo, and to add some clay to the front for balance and a string of firecrackers to the rear for a fuse.

The fireworks and dancing lasted until the sun went down and the moon came up. As soon as the moon took over from the sun, everyone began heading back home for dinner and bed. Unfortunately, the last bus to Chinghung had already gone by on the highway, but one of the villagers invited me to his house, where I was treated to a meal of water buffalo meat. My host said the Tai only ate water buffalo on special occasions, but I never found out exactly what the occasion was—just that it was in honor of a monk who had lived in Hsishuangbanna a long time ago, that it was held at certain villages in the region on the second full moon of the year, and that it lasted three days. Since it was a Buddhist festival, it didn't involve drinking, and I woke up the next morning without the usual hangover. After thanking my hosts, I walked back out to the main road and hitched a ride to the next town in the back of a truck. After I finally caught a bus back to Chinghung, I recuperated on the veranda again and spent the rest of the day planning my next adventure.

茶

21. Tea

I HAD ALREADY MADE excursions north of Chinghung, east of Chinghung, and south of Chinghung. It was time to head west. And the next
morning there was a bus heading in that direction. It was the tea tour
bus, which began by following the main road west thirty-five kilometers, after which it turned off onto a side road and drove another eight
into the countryside to the small village of Nannuoshan. The village had
grown up around what the Chinese called the King of Tea Trees.

While most tea trees are grown close to the ground to make picking
leaves easier, the king was nearly six meters high, and botanists estimated it was over eight hundred years old. The reason it was so big was
that it had been abandoned centuries before and allowed to grow on its
own. Its discovery thirty years earlier lent support to the theory that tea
was introduced into China and to the rest of the world from Hsishuangbanna and the region just across the border in Burma.

According to my now-departed friend John Blofeld, the Chinese first
began drinking tea 1,700 years ago, when they boiled the leaves to make
a tonic. It wasn't until later that it was drunk by itself. And it wasn't
until about 1,000 years ago that it replaced other herbal brews in China
as the beverage of choice. Despite the subsequent spread of tea growing
throughout other areas in China, the teas of Yunnan are considered
unique in terms of their health benefits, and many elderly Chinese insist
on their daily pot of p'u-er tea. P'u-er is the name of a town on the road
between Kunming and Chinghung where the teas of Hsishuangbanna

are prepared for distribution to Tibet and the rest of China, and the name has become synonymous with teas from the whole region. But the home of p'u-er tea was actually the area around Nannuoshan, where tourists can visit the lone survivor of an 800-year-old tea plantation. I should note that the king had been dethroned about ten years before my arrival when researchers found a thirty-four-meter-high, wild tea tree on Taheishan west of Menghai and estimated its age at 1,700 years, or twice that of the king.

Unfortunately, Taheishan happened to be on the Burmese border, and foreigners weren't allowed to visit that area without first going through a gauntlet of red tape and handing out an appropriate amount of money. But Menghai itself was an open town, and that was the tea tour's next and final destination. Most foreigners passed through Menghai only long enough to change buses or hitchhike out of town, but it had become the center of tea production in the region, and I joined two dozen others aboard the tea tour in sampling some of the area's teas. The most famous, of course, was p'u-er with its distinctive musty flavor, which sometimes tastes like liquid dirt. But Menghai also produces black teas and green teas and even a white-tipped tea known as Silver Needle. I tried them all and bought as much as my bag would hold. When the tea tour finally headed back to Chinghung, I walked out to the road and caught the next bus heading in the opposite direction.

Sixteen kilometers later, I got off at the village of Chingchen. I wanted to visit Hsishuangbanna's most unusual pagoda. It was built on top of a man-made hill, and instead of being round or square like other pagodas, it was eight-sided. And it was made not of stone, but of wood. It was a masterpiece of construction, which became more evident as I used my binoculars to study the details of the carvings and the artistic motifs that lined its outside all the way to the top of its twenty-meter-high spire. According to a sign in the courtyard, the pagoda was first built in 1701 and had recently been rebuilt after being destroyed during the Cultural Revolution.

Near the pagoda there was also a wooden shrine hall. Several young monks were sitting outside on the steps flicking lighters and waiting for

Entrance of Chingchen's eight-sided pagoda

Village well in Chingchen

the old monks to call them inside to begin class. In the dirt courtyard between the pagoda and the shrine hall, I saw a huge hollow tree that was putting out new leaves. I asked the young monks what kind of tree it was, but they just kept flicking their lighters. Like the hollow tree, Buddhism was still putting forth new leaves in Hsishuangbanna, but I had no idea what kind of fruit.

After failing to satisfy my curiosity about the tree, I walked over to the pagoda and heard this story from the lady who sold entry tickets. The pagoda was located just outside the village of Chingchen, and a long time ago, the ruler of Chingchen had a daughter named Nan-mu-han, whom he married to Chao-han, the son of the ruler of Mengche, which was a few kilometers to the west. Well, the ruler of Mengche was a greedy man, and he decided to invade the territory of Chingchen. Chao-han overheard his father's plan, and he told his wife. To keep word about his plan from leaking out, the ruler of Mengche had forbidden anyone to leave the palace. But Nan-mu-han was a clever girl, and she wrote a letter to her father, put it inside a dried gourd, and wrote her father's name on the outside of the gourd. And during the night she dropped the gourd into the river that flowed through Mengche on its way past Chingchen. Sure enough, the next morning an old woman washing clothes along the riverbank in Chingchen saw the gourd and took it to her father, and he opened it and learned about his neighboring ruler's intentions. And when the ruler of Mengche invaded, he was defeated.

When I asked the old lady when all that happened, she told me there used to be a memorial marker on the road outside Mengche, but it disappeared a long time ago. Words, though, outlast stone, and she told me that the villagers of Chingchen and Mengche had been reciting that story for the past two hundred years, ever since it was put into a song called "The Gourd Letter."

I thanked the old lady for telling me the story and considered my next move, which was to call it a day and spend the night at a hostel back in Menghai. It turned out I was there on Saturday, and the most famous public market in all of Hsishuangbanna took place Sunday

Broomsellers at the Sunday market in Menghan

morning south of Menghai in Menghan. I couldn't possibly miss such an event and I boarded the early-morning bus, which left Menghai just after seven, and arrived at the market before eight. I thought maybe I would be getting there early, but I was already late. Thousands of villagers crowded what was simply an intersection of dirt roads. I soon disappeared in their midst.

Among the items that caught my attention and my cash were hand-woven Tai cotton tube skirts selling for 2 dollars apiece and packages of a dozen Burmese cigars selling for 1 dollar. Yao women were asking the same price for three packets of opium. I had already visited the Yao in the mountains of northern Kuanghsi province, but these Yao were from the mountains along the China-Burma border, which apparently was not all that easy to police. The idea of buying some opium certainly occurred to me, but I couldn't very well smoke it while I was traveling. And taking it back to Hong Kong could have been a problem. Besides, the price of high-grade heroin in Hong Kong was only 15 bucks for just as much.

After two hours of struggling through the throng, I returned to the bus. It wasn't due to return to Menghai for another hour, but I had seen enough, and bought enough. According to the driver, the Menghan market was overrated. He said the Sunday market at Talo to the west was even better. But Talo was off-limits to foreigners. It was on the border. He said the hot imports there were nylon mosquito nets from Thailand, skirt material, and cosmetics, while the most popular Chinese exports were hot-water bottles, plastic shoes, flashlights, and lighters, the popularity of which I had already noted among the young monks in Chingchen. I told him that I was happy with my tube skirts and cigars, but that I regretted not being able to visit any Pulang villages. The mention of the Pulang got his attention.

布朗族

22. The Pulang

ONE OF THE PLACES I was hoping to visit in Hsishuangbanna was Pulang Mountain—the ancient home of the Pulang people. At last count, there were eighty-two thousand Pulang living in China, and most of them were living on and around Pulang Mountain, southeast of Menghai. The Pulang have been living there for as long as anyone can remember. According to Chinese historians, their ancestors were living there as early as two thousand years ago. Over the centuries, the Pulang have developed close relationships with other ethnic groups in the area, especially the Tai, and many of their religious and social customs are linked with those of the Tai.

For example, the Pulang have no written language of their own, so they send their children to live as monks in Tai temples for several years to learn the Tai script. And many of their religious festivals are the same as those of the Tai, the most important of which are the Door Closing and the Door Opening festivals, which have been tied to the early development of Buddhism 2,500 years ago.

In ancient India, Buddhist monks held a three-month retreat during the summer rainy season to concentrate on their spiritual practice, and the Tai and Pulang have adapted that custom to their own more secular needs. From the middle of July to the middle of October, no villager is allowed to go further than the local market. It isn't just the rainy season, it's also the farming season, and everyone is needed to help with the rice crop. Hence, the Pulang sing Tai songs to celebrate closing their doors, and they sing Tai songs when they open them up again.

While I was complaining to the driver about the border restrictions that prevented me from learning more about the Pulang, he surprised me. It turned out he was Tai, and he knew all about the Pulang. He was married to one. He even showed me a photo in his wallet. She was lovely and not what I expected. She didn't look at all like a toad.

Since the bus wasn't leaving for another hour, he confirmed a story I had read earlier. It turns out a long time ago the rain god P'a-ya-t'ien didn't send down any rain on Pulang Mountain for seven years. The toads that inhabited the mountain couldn't take it anymore, and one of them went to Heaven and got into a fight with P'a-ya-t'ien—and got thrown out of Heaven. But this was a determined toad, and the toad went to his friend the termite and asked for help. The toad flew back in secret one night on the termite's back and stole P'a-ya-t'ien's weapons. Then the next day he challenged P'a-ya-t'ien to a fight. When P'a-ya-t'ien discovered his weapons were gone, he had no choice but to give up and promise to send down rain every summer.

But that was only half the story. Earlier, before the toad flew up to Heaven on the termite's back, to make himself lighter, he took off his skin and left it at home. While he was gone, his wife thought it was just an old, smelly robe, and she threw it into the fire. Thus, when he later returned in triumph, the toad husband was unable to resume his original form and had to make do with a body without warts. The Pulang people have been happy with the outcome ever since, as was my Tai bus driver.

Even though I couldn't visit the mountain where all this happened, hearing the driver recount what happened there long ago was enough. Before long, the bus filled up, and we returned to Menghai. It was time once again to head back to Chinghung, but I decided to visit one more village on the way there that I had heard about. Halfway to Chinghung, I got off at a place along the Liusha River. On the other side of the river was the Aini village of Panla. There was a bridge, but it was only two bamboos wide. Fortunately, there was a rope to hang on to, and I was able to tightrope my way across above the Liusha's surging brown waters.

Panla was your typical Aini village of dirt and wood and big pigs and small people, except for one thing. Almost every house had clumps of orchids growing on the roof. It was a transforming touch, and the villagers were hospitable. As soon as I entered the village, one of the women invited me into her house for a cup of tea, and I sat down and learned more Aini words. One of the words I learned was "ao-ma la-na." "Ao-ma la-na" is the Aini word for "black rice."

When I was in Chinghung I ate black rice with every meal and thought it the best rice I had ever tasted. It had such a nutty flavor, I could have eaten it by itself. The local authorities also realized their rice was something special, and I had heard that it was illegal to take it out of Hsishuangbanna. When I told this to my Aini host, she disappeared and came back a few minutes later with a bag of ao-ma la-na seeds. I really wasn't planning on becoming a rice farmer, but I couldn't say no. I also couldn't say no to the embroidery she showed me.

And so I returned to Chinghung loaded down with black rice seeds and more embroidery. People who visited Chinghung a few years before me likened the town to an easy-going tropical backwater. That image was history. The new airport delivered several hundred tourists every day from Kunming. And a couple dozen buses brought even more visitors via the long, winding highway that took two days. But even though Chinghung was on a building binge, all the new hotels still aren't enough in April. In the middle of that month, the Tai celebrate the end of the old year and the beginning of the new one. The Chinese call it the Water-Splashing Festival, and there isn't a hotel room in town or even a seat on the two-day bus.

As for what all the excitement was about, well, a long time ago, back when humankind first began to populate this region, it was ruled by an evil demon. The evil demon had seven beautiful wives, and the youngest resented the way her husband treated the people. One night, after she got the demon drunk, she pretended concern about her husband's health and found out that his weak spot was his neck. When the demon fell asleep, she took one of his long, white hairs and wrapped it around his neck and pulled with all her might. The demon's head was sliced clean off and rolled onto the floor. But instead of just sitting there, the head began to spout blood and fire—and the blood and fire began to spread. The seventh wife called the other wives, and they all poured water over the head to wash away the blood and put out the fire. Thus, they finally freed the people from the demon's wicked rule. And ever since then, the Tai have washed away their sins of the past year by splashing water on each other—and anyone in their vicinity.

That was the origin of the Water-Splashing Festival, and it was celebrated every year throughout Hsishuangbanna around the middle of April to coincide with the beginning of the Tai lunar calendar—that is, it was until the local officials decided it wouldn't do to have the festival changing dates every year. So several years before my visit the government decreed that the Tai festival would henceforth be celebrated between April 13 and April 15. The weather in Chinghung had turned hot, and I could have used a good splashing, but the festival was still several weeks away, and I had other plans.

I passed up the experience of the two-day bus ride back to Kunming and headed to the airport instead. I had booked a ticket on a flight back the day I arrived, and I planned to continue on from Kunming to Dali. When I first looked at a map, I could see that there was a road between Chinghung and Dali. But it was a three-day trip by bus, and foreigners weren't allowed on that particular road anyway. I never found out why. Opium traffic? Military secrets? Embarrassing road conditions? No cold beer? While I was waiting for my plane to take me back to Kunming, I met a pair of Dutch travelers who had tried to hitchhike the road to Dali. They said that halfway there they were picked up by the police and spent a couple days in a local jail before being sent back to Chinghung. The only bus foreigners could take out of Chinghung was the one back to Kunming, the one that took two days. And so I left Hsishuangbanna and spent one last night at the Camellia Hotel in the City of Eternal Spring.

彝族

23. The Yi

THE NEXT MORNING, I began my northward journey at the Kunming long-distance bus station. The bus to Dali left on time, and before long I was cruising down what had to be the most modern highway in Southwest China. Unfortunately, it only lasted thirty-five kilometers, until the town of Anning.

Anning is the home of the Anning hot springs, and it has been on the itinerary of travelers ever since it came to their attention two thousand years ago. The road I was traveling on, it turned out, was part of what was once called the Southern Silk Road. It was never as popular as the northern route through Central Asia, but it saw a steady stream of merchants and monks. And what traveler wouldn't welcome a good soak? But the bus I was on didn't stop in Anning. Alas, the modern (i.e., smooth) highway did. The distance between Kunming and Dali was four hundred kilometers, and the driver was determined to get there before nightfall, regardless of whether the road was smooth or not. The only time we stopped, other than for the occasional pee break, was for lunch in the town of Chuhsiung. Chuhsiung was in the heart of Yi country. The Yi made up the largest minority in Yunnan, with over three million members as of 1990. And their biggest concentration was in the mountains around Chuhsiung. While my fellow passengers filed out of the bus and into a restaurant for lunch, I strolled down the street to the town's main bookstore, such as it was, and bought a small book that recounted the Yi story of how we all got here.

Yi tribesman selling firewood

According to the Yi, or at least the account in the book, humankind passed through three ages. The first was apparently an experiment. The gods created people with a single eye in the middle of their chest. But these early people were so dumb, they didn't know how to grow vegetables or grains or even how to make babies. Eventually, the gods got tired of the experiment and sent down a heat wave that killed all the one-eyed people.

During the second age, the gods tried another prototype with two eyes, but with the eyes set vertically, one above the other, in the middle of the head. These two-eyed people were more intelligent. They finally figured out how babies were made, and they started propagating like rabbits. Even brothers and sisters made babies. But they were always getting into fights over mates, and the gods got fed up with their lack of morality and sent down a flood to wash the earth clean. As the floodwaters started to rise, the gods sent down an emissary to see if there wasn't one kindhearted person among the vertical-eyed people worth saving.

But while the emissary was searching, he was captured by three brothers, who refused to release him until he told them how to survive the flood. The emissary wasn't about to help such selfish people, and he told the eldest brother that the only way to survive the flood was aboard an iron boat. The eldest brother smiled and went to build his boat, but neither he nor the other brothers set the emissary free. So the emissary told the second brother that the only way to survive was aboard a bronze boat, and off the brother went to build his bronze boat, again leaving the emissary still tied up.

The third brother wasn't as cruel as his two elder brothers, and he set the emissary free. In thanks, the emissary gave him a magic seed and told him to plant it in the ground. When he did, it immediately produced a huge gourd. The emissary told the youngest brother to climb inside the gourd with his sister. And just as they did, the floodwaters rushed into their village, sweeping over their two stupid brothers but carrying the younger brother and sister to safety to start a new race of people.

Several weeks earlier when I was in Hsishuangbanna, I encountered the Chinuo story of the brother and sister who survived the great flood inside a huge drum, the problem they had afterwards overcoming the prohibition against incest, and about how they eventually gave up trying to have children but found a gourd inside of which were the ancestors of the four major tribes that still live in that area. At least that was the Chinuo story.

The Yi tell it like this: after the flood the vertical-eyed brother and sister climbed out of their gourd and realized they were the only people left. They also realized that despite the prohibition against incest, they would have to have children. After several false starts, the sister finally gave birth to a gourd. When she and her brother opened up the gourd, they found thirty-six children, each of them with horizontal eyes, just like you and me. Each of these children became the ancestor of a different tribe. And thus began the third age of humankind.

About the time I came to the end of this story, my fellow passengers filed out of the restaurant, climbed back on board the bus, and waved for me to join them, completely unaware that we were all descended from a pair of incestuous, vertical-eyed people who gave birth to a gourd. As I returned to my seat I couldn't help wondering if there was a fourth age on the horizon.

鷄足山

24. Chickenfoot Mountain

Fᴿᴏᴍ Cʜᴜʜsɪᴜɴɢ we wound our way up and down a series of plateaus, then down and across an equal number of plains. It was late March, and the landscape was a dozen shades of brown and red, with the occasional green or yellow patch of winter wheat or rapeseed. It was already late afternoon when we crossed the Hsiangyun Plain, where farmers have been plowing the reddish-brown topsoil for the last three thousand years.

During World War II, there was an airstrip on the plain where the Flying Tigers stopped to unload their cargo and refuel after crossing the Burma Hump. The old runway was now being readied to handle passenger flights, which would cut travel time between Kunming and Dali from ten hours to less than two. But no one on the bus could tell me when flights would begin. A new highway was also being built that was expected to cut travel time for vehicles to five or six hours.

We made it to Dali in a little less than ten. Well, actually, we didn't make it to Dali. The old Dali of a thousand years ago was another fifteen kilometers to the north. It was now called Dali Township. I was in Dali City, which was the new name for what used to be called Hsiakuan, meaning "below the pass." Half the signs in town, though, still said ʜsɪᴀᴋᴜᴀɴ, so as far as I was concerned, I was in Hsiakuan. And I was walking down the main street of Hsiakuan as the sun was going down and looking for a place to stay, when I ran into two Tibetan men decked out in leather coats and boots and fur hats. Spread out on a cloth in front of them was one of the strangest-looking things I had ever seen. It was a tiger penis. At least that was what they said it was. It had to be one of the animal kingdom's strangest solutions for procreation. It was coiled up like a snake and easily two feet long, and the first six inches below the head were lined with dozens of long, fleshy spines angled toward the base. Apparently they inflated or at least stiffened during intercourse, making coitus interruptus impossible. Unbelievable. What will the gods think of next? I was so amazed, I didn't ask the price. No doubt they were hoping to sell the penis for use in an elixir to enhance sexual potency. I was too tired to think about my sex life and passed up the opportunity of a lifetime. I asked them instead where I might find a good hotel. They recommended the Erhai Guesthouse. Feeling a bit tired—too tired to walk there—I flagged down a pedicab, and a few minutes later I checked in.

The guesthouse was old, but it was still the best place to stay in Hsiakuan. The rooms were huge, and there was laundry service and hot water every night. Also, it was discretely located inside a vast compound away from the street. The guesthouse even had its own doctor, and I had a cold and wasn't feeling well, especially after the ten-hour bus ride from Kunming. The doctor came up to my room and gave me an hour-long acupressure massage and some medicine. The next morning my cold was gone. At 50RMB, or nearly 10 bucks, it was the most expensive massage I had had in China (this was in 1992), but it was worth every RMB.

I forgot to mention that when I arrived in Hsiakuan, I went inside the bus station and bought a ticket on the morning bus to Pinchuan for the following day—and when I woke up, it was the following day. Pinchuan used to be off-limits to foreigners, but those restrictions had been lifted. I left my bag at the hotel and told them I would be back in two days. Outside the hotel, a pedicab was waiting, just for me it seemed, and I arrived at the bus station ten minutes early, just in time to load up on er-k'uai. Er-k'uai must be a Hsiakuan specialty. I've never seen them anywhere else in China. The outside is made of dough, and they are shaped like a half-moon and are about six inches long. They look like a pasty or a large tart and are filled with deep-fried fritters and black sesame paste and a couple of other things I couldn't identify. They made a fine morning snack, and I should have bought a few more for the trail. But the bus was waiting, and the next one wasn't due to leave until noon.

Our departure was memorable. There were half a dozen other buses lined up inside the station parking lot, and all of them were scheduled to leave at the same time. The station bell rang, and they began peeling out, one behind the other, while the entire station staff stood at attention in the middle of the parking lot and looked on. All the drivers honked, and we rode out onto the main street on a crescendo of horns. We were off, off for the town of Pinchuan, seventy kilometers of bad road to the northeast. Pinchuan was the gateway to my next destination: Chickenfoot Mountain. Don't let the name put you off. Chickenfoot is the most famous pilgrimage site in Southwest China. And it felt good to be a pilgrim again.

South of Hsiakuan, the bus turned off onto a narrow cobblestone road and rumbled through fields of knee-high beans and winter wheat, fruit orchards in bloom, and the occasional village of traditional Pai houses with their chest-high granite foundations, whitewashed walls, timbered second storeys, and tiled roofs.

The Pai and their ancestors have been living in western Yunnan for at least three thousand years, and the succession of Pai states that once ruled the area provided Southwest China with its most advanced early civilization. Driving through their villages was like driving through well-off Chinese farming villages, except that Pai women still wore their traditional clothing: long pants partly covered in front by an embroidered apron, a long-sleeved white shirt partly covered by a sleeveless blue tunic that buttoned at the left shoulder, and bands of embroidered material wrapped around the head. The impression was one of simplicity and elegance, and these were farmers.

The bus finally climbed past their fields and villages and crossed a series of barren ridges in desperate need of trees. Two hours after leaving Hsiakuan, we finally pulled into Pinchuan. Although Pinchuan was one of the ancient centers of early Pai civilization, it wasn't much of a town. It was more of a village. For me it was just another place worth staying in only long enough to catch a bus out of it. Imagine my dismay when I learned the next bus to Chickenfoot Mountain didn't leave for another three hours.

The only place of interest in Pinchuan was the traffic circle at the center of town, and it didn't take me long to get bored sitting there watching the occasional farm vehicle or motorcycle circle around and disappear. Finally, I walked down the street to where the weekly market was being held and talked to the drivers of several trucks being loaded with produce. I was in luck: one of them was going halfway to Chickenfoot Mountain, and I joined a dozen Pai villagers and a ton of vegetables in the back of the truck. A few minutes later, we were on our way.

Every once in a while, the truck stopped to lighten its load, and I got a chance to watch several village activities, including the various stages of house construction. The most interesting part was how the Pai made their walls. They set down a wooden wall form on top of the house's granite foundation, then filled the form with dirt, and then tamped the dirt down until it was hard. Once one level was finished, they moved the form up and repeated the process. When they were done, they covered the wall's surface with a layer of plaster, then painted it white. It looked as hard as cement.

The truck finally dropped me and everyone else off at the village of Tientou. It was Tuesday, which turned out to be market day in Tientou, too, and the market was jammed with people down from the hills to trade all manner of things. While I was checking out the market, one man came up to me and offered me a young owl. He wanted 30RMB, or 6 dollars, for the bird. I asked him what he expected me to do with an owl. He said, "Eat it." I looked at the owl, and the owl looked at me. I blinked first.

In addition to local Pai villagers from Tientou and neighboring villages, the market was packed with black-turbaned Yi down from the surrounding mountains to sell firewood, medicinal herbs, and animal skins. Their donkeys were waiting at the edge of the marketplace to

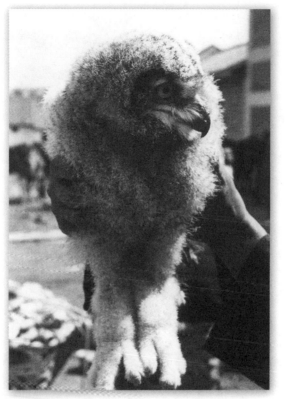

Baby owl for sale

carry back kerosene, cooking oil, farm tools, and—what was this?—a metal box about the size of a bedside radio with big red lights, a few buttons, and a switch. The sign on top said, THE RAT DESTROYER: JUST FLICK THE SWITCH, AND YOUR RAT PROBLEMS ARE OVER. Apparently it emitted a high-frequency signal that rats found annoying. It probably just drove them next door to the neighbor's house. But I wondered where an Yi villager was going to get electricity. Maybe someone in their village had a generator

After strolling through the market, I walked back to the dirt road. Once again, I was in luck. There was a truck full of market produce and Pai villagers, and it was headed for the village of Shachih, which was located between the toes of Chickenfoot Mountain and was as far as the road went. When I asked if I could hitch a ride, someone reached

Market day in Pinchuan

down and helped me climb aboard. A few minutes later, we were off. It was a bad road, and the driver constantly had to slow down to a crawl to keep from breaking an axle crossing the irrigation ditches that local farmers dug across the road without concern for vehicle traffic. An hour later, we were there. When I originally joined the other villagers on the truck, I thought I was hitching a ride. It turned out I was a paying passenger, as was everyone else who made use of this convenient form of transport. Public buses on the road to Shachih were about as frequent as meals—speaking of which, it was that time again.

After paying 5RMB for the ride, I walked up the muddy street that led through Shachih and decided to have lunch at one of the small restaurants that lined the village's one and only road. These Pai restaurants were lovely little places, with open-air, garden-like settings—very different from their more commercial counterparts at the feet of other sacred mountains I had visited. I chose one on the left that had dozens of potted geraniums and snapdragons and hollyhocks and even sweet williams. It was a good choice, and I had a memorable meal, highlighted by scrambled eggs with slices of cured wild boar meat. The meat was better than the best Canadian bacon I had eaten, and now I understood why Asterix's friend Obelix was always singing the praises of wild boar. The whole meal, which included a large plate of vegetables along with soup and rice, cost 12RMB, or slightly more than 2 dollars.

While I talked with the Pai woman who ran the restaurant, I looked at the faded painting of Chickenfoot Mountain on her wall showing the location of many of the 108 Buddhist temples and shrines that had covered the mountain's slopes before the Cultural Revolution. I asked her how many were left. She said, "Three." Chickenfoot Mountain, or Chitzushan, had once been the most famous Buddhist pilgrimage site in all of Southwest China. And despite the destruction wrought by the Red Guards, it was once again attracting a new stream of pilgrims, many of whom hired buses to bring them there from as far away as Kunming or Chengtu. Clearly, I arrived during the slack season. As I started up the trail, I found myself alone. It was late afternoon, and I began to wonder where those three temples were.

Old map of the temples on Chickenfoot Mountain

I don't know who started calling it Chickenfoot Mountain or when, but everyone I talked to agreed the mountain's name came from the shape of its ridges, which look like the claws of a giant chicken. Apparently, the leg and the rest of the chicken are somewhere up there in the clouds. The summit is 3,200 meters above sea level, or 1,500 meters above the surrounding plain where I started out. The woman at the restaurant said it was a five-hour hike, and about the same on horseback. I walked past a string of a dozen horses and mules at the entrance all saddled up and waiting to take pilgrims like me to the summit for a measly 20RMB, or 4 dollars. I considered it. The price was right. But this was supposed to be a sacred mountain. I felt it deserved my sweat, and it didn't take long before I was venerating the stone steps with my modest offering.

The steps were at odd intervals and definitely not made for your normal human stride. More likely the distance and height between them were made with horses and mules in mind. As I plodded along, I passed an old man digging a drainage ditch beside the trail. He had a long beard and wasn't wearing a shirt, and he greeted me with a wide smile. He

Chickenfoot Mountain's claws

said I had better hurry if I wanted to reach Chusheng Temple before the rain began. I looked up and saw nothing but blue sky. I asked him what made him think it was going to rain. He said he smelled it in the wind. I sniffed, but the only thing I smelled was my sweat.

An hour later, Chusheng Temple came into view where the trail leveled off. Where it did, there was a hollow tree, the base of which had been converted into a shrine. I lit some incense and paid my respects, and looked up to see if the old mantis was still around. A long time ago there was a mantis that lived in the tree's branches. But it was no ordinary mantis. It was huge, and it could change itself into human form. The form it usually chose was that of a beautiful woman. Because the weather on Chickenfoot Mountain was so changeable, many lonely travelers were forced to take refuge in the tree's hollow, especially when a beautiful woman beckoned. But when they did, the woman grabbed them in her vice-like grip and drained them of their bodily fluids.

This went on for many years, until one day about seven hundred years ago a monk by the name of Chu-ch'eng heard about the mantis and resolved to do something about it. He walked up to the tree, and, as

Tree shrine on the way to Chusheng temple

usual, the mantis was waiting inside in the guise of a beautiful woman. Chu-ch'eng ignored her, sat down inside the tree's hollow, and began to chant a mantra, or magic spell, and immediately the woman was changed back into a mantis. The mantis tried to grab the monk, but the monk chanted another mantra, and the mantis became dizzy and collapsed. When it recovered, the monk was still there. The mantis then bowed down and asked to become the monk's disciple. The mantis studied with the monk for many years and eventually became enlightened. Since I didn't know any mantras, I bowed as quickly as I could, then looked up at the branches, just in case. No mantis. But as I looked up, it began to rain, as the old man had predicted. I didn't linger and hurried up the trail to the temple.

A few minutes later, I was there. Chusheng is the largest temple on the mountain and the only major temple that escaped the sledgehammers of the Red Guards. It was first built 350 years ago, but it didn't assume its present form or name until the beginning of the twentieth century. During my journey the previous year in the region known as South of the Yangtze, I visited Yunchushan, where the monk Hsu-yun, or Empty Cloud, died in 1959 at the age of 120. Empty Cloud was the first president of the Buddhist Association of China and the most famous Zen master of the last few centuries. He came to Chickenfoot Mountain in 1906 at the age of 67 with the intention of restoring the temple there. And he didn't come empty-handed. He brought with him an endowment from the empress dowager, Tzu Hsi. And the first of the temples he rebuilt was Chusheng, or Thank God Temple—the god being the empress dowager.

As I entered, I walked past two huge cedars, then two huge wooden guardians almost as big as the trees—Heng and Ha again. I continued through the front courtyard, past a cherry tree in glorious bloom, and past the drum tower on the left and the bell tower on the right to the main shrine hall, where I met the abbot. He was a kindly old man, who kept rushing around the whole time I was there. There weren't many monks, and he had a lot of responsibilities, one of which was to take

Statues of Heng and Ha outside Chusheng Temple

care of guests. He invited me to spend the night, and I gladly accepted. The summit was still four hours away, and it was already four o'clock. Besides, I wasn't too sure about accommodations along the rest of the trail. The abbot showed me to a room and gave me a thermos of hot water, and I enjoyed a rare afternoon cup of instant coffee. Around six o'clock, he came by again to call me to dinner, and I enjoyed an equally good vegetarian meal. That night I fell asleep listening to the temple bell and the wind—just like old times, when I lived in a monastery in Taiwan.

My reverie came to an end early the next morning. It was four hours to the summit, and I hoped to make it there and back to Chusheng by dusk. At least that was my plan. It didn't take long for me to be distracted. Less than three hundred meters past the temple, I turned off the trail and followed a sign that pointed down a slope to a pavilion where I had an unobstructed view of Jade Dragon Waterfall. A long time ago, a monk by the name of Chih-kuang lived on Chickenfoot Mountain. Chih-kuang was no ordinary monk. He had magic powers, and he had friends among the immortals.

One day Chih-kuang sent an invitation to his friends to attend a banquet, and one of those he invited was the King of Jade Dragon Snowy Mountain. When the king came he brought with him his youngest daughter, Jade Dragon Waterfall. While her father and Chih-kuang regaled themselves with rare delicacies and stories of their most recent exploits among the clouds and in far-off lands, the princess went wandering through the forest. She came to the very spot where I was standing, and she fell in love with its scenic beauty. When it was time to leave, she asked her father if she could stay a while longer, and he agreed. Chih-kuang then gave her that piece of land for her own, and she never returned to her father's palace in the Snowy Mountains to the north. Instead, she spent her days singing with the wind and dancing with the flowers, and she used her own magic powers to build temples and shrines in the vicinity. Over time, she grew younger and more beautiful, until finally she turned into a clear stream. A thousand years later, I gazed at her thin, graceful form as it turned to mist and gathered itself again at the bottom of Jade Dragon Waterfall.

After lingering as long as I dared, I returned to the trail and found myself enthralled by the trail itself, as it led through a forest of rhododendrons in full bloom. They were gloriously red, fire-engine red, Vamp-of-Savannah lipstick red. A spray of them had broken off and were lying on the trail, and I couldn't ignore the gift of the gods. I picked them up and stuck them behind my ear. Just then, I saw an animal dart across the trail and disappear into the forest. It was bigger than a dog, but smaller than a sheep. It had a tail and brown fur, and I wondered if it was a friend or perhaps a relative of the wild boar whose meat I ate before starting up the trail. Since the animal was obviously more afraid of me than I was of it, I shrugged and continued up the mountain, shielded from the sun by conifers and broad-leaved evergreens and hundreds of red rhododendrons and pink and white and even yellow azaleas in bloom. It was late March and a glorious time to be on the mountain.

Walking along the mountain's carpet of colored petals, I met a Tibetan monk wrapped in maroon robes coming down the trail. As he approached, I chanted the Tibetan mantra: "Om, mani padme hum," meaning "O, Jewel in the Lotus." He responded with a longer mantra, which I didn't understand but which he said would guarantee my safety for the rest of my journey. He said he had been a monk ever since he was a little boy, and he had lived for many years at Taer Lamasery in the province of Chinghai. I told him I had visited Taer the previous year during my trek to the source of the Yellow River. But reaching the source of the Yellow River suddenly seemed easy. He said he was ninety-four. Yes, ninety-four years old, and he had just hiked to the 3,200-meter summit of Chickenfoot Mountain, and now he was hiking down, and he wasn't even breathing hard. Om, mani padme hum.

Not long after meeting the monk, I arrived at Huiteng Nunnery. The nunnery was located directly below the summit, which was visible far above, jutting through the clouds. In front of the nunnery, someone had set up several reclining bamboo chairs so that visitors could rest up for the final push and at the same time view the peak and the pagoda on top toward which they were heading. It was a beautiful view. The nunnery itself was much smaller than Chusheng Temple, but it included a dozen rooms for pilgrims, and I think if I ever visit Chickenfoot again, this will be where I'll stay. It was only two and a half hours from the foot of the trail, and the atmosphere was much more intimate, if I can say that about a nunnery. There were also several shacks outside the front gate serving tea and a few simple dishes, such as wild boar and mushrooms.

After a brief rest, I pressed on and began the final ascent. On the way, I passed a string of mules struggling up the uneven stone steps with packs of bricks and grain. After less than an hour, I came to the ruins of Copper Buddha Temple and entered its small rebuilt shrine hall. Inside, a young monk was singing an ode to Kuan-yin, the Bodhisattva of Compassion. He was oblivious to my presence, and I left him that way. A sign outside on the left announced another famous sight on the mountain: Huashoumen, or Great Glory Gate. The sign pointed to a side trail, and I followed it through a narrow archway. Another sign said, THE BIG VIEW IS UP AHEAD. I stumbled forward a few more feet and found myself face to face with the gate to eternity. The gate, however, was not the kind of gate I expected. It turned out to be a cliff face

Huashoumen

of black rock where the natural faulting of the rock had formed a gate. That was the last place Kashyapa was seen.

Kashyapa was one of the Buddha's greatest disciples, and he reportedly came to Chickenfoot Mountain 2,400 years ago. To understand Kashyapa's importance, it's necessary to go back to when Brahma, the Lord of Creation, offered the Buddha a flower and asked him to preach the Dharma. The Buddha took the flower and held it up. His devotees and disciples were puzzled—all except Kashyapa, who smiled. This marked the beginning of Zen: the direct transmission of understanding with a flower and a smile. Kashyapa thus became the First Patriarch of Zen in India. Though there are no records attesting to it, Kashyapa was said to have come to Chickenfoot Mountain following the Buddha's Nirvana. And he took up residence in a cave below Huashoumen.

Not long after Kashyapa moved here, two monks came up the trail one day, and when they reached Kashyapa's cave, he came outside and said he hadn't eaten in months and asked if they had any food. When they said they only had enough for themselves, Kashyapa went back inside his cave, and the walls of the cliff closed behind him. He hasn't been seen since. When the two monks realized their mistake, they cried in front of the cliff, and they finally cried themselves to death. There was a small well at the base of the cliff still full of their tears. I had read that pilgrims scooped out the water and splashed it in their eyes to cure cataracts and other eye disorders. I splashed some in my eyes, too, and the clouds overhead cleared.

As I looked up, I could see the pagoda directly above me. I was almost there. A few minutes later, I was. I was out of breath, but before me was the pagoda. It was surrounded by a small temple and a series of shabby, privately run hostels that catered to overnight visitors. One of the highlights of a visit to Chickenfoot Mountain is said to be the sunrise. On clear days, visitors can supposedly see the blue waters of Erhai Lake to the west and the 5,500-meter crest of Jade Dragon Snowy Mountain to the north. But the clear sky suddenly turned to swirling mist. It was cold, and I wasn't about to spend the night. But I was hungry. I went inside one of the huts that crowded together behind the pagoda, and

I ordered a bowl of noodles. One of the mule team drivers was also inside, and he invited me to join him in a glass of liquid heat. He dipped an empty glass into a huge jar that contained some kind of grain alcohol and slices of papaya. I don't know what the purpose of the papaya was. All I tasted was fire. But it was a good fire. The mule driver said he got 11RMB, or 2 dollars, for each load of food or building materials he brought up and 20RMB when he carried a person up to the summit. It was a tough life, but at least there was something waiting at the summit. After a few glasses of papaya spirits, I felt as light as a cloud.

Before heading back down, I paused to pay my respects at the square pagoda that rose forty meters above the small stone courtyard of Chin-ting Temple. The pagoda dates back to the middle of the seventh century, when Buddhism first began to flourish on the mountain. It has remained the symbol of Chickenfoot Mountain ever since. After paying my respects, I flew down the steps, and in less than an hour I found myself back at Huiteng Nunnery. This time, instead of continuing back down the way I had come, I turned off on a side trail that led to the nearby ruins of Fangkuang Temple. Along the way, I spotted a pheasant hopping in the bushes. It was the most gorgeous pheasant I had ever seen. It had a long white tail and a blue body. But when it saw me, it disappeared. A few minutes later, I came to the ruins, which were buried beneath the grass of a large meadow. Before the Red Guards destroyed the place, pilgrims came here to see the mysterious light that appeared once a year above the temple.

I lay down on the grass and looked up and watched the clouds drift by. I recorded everything I had seen earlier on my way up the mountain on my tape recorder. I don't use a notebook and pencil anymore. The previous Christmas, my friend Fred Goforth had given me a voice recorder, and it is all I ever use now. My memory is as bad as the wind's. But with my handy-dandy voice recorder, I could record two hours of action-packed episodes of my daily life on one little cassette. At Fangkuang Temple, I even recorded the shape of the clouds. I saw one that looked like a bear and decided that it must have been what I saw crossing the trail earlier.

Chinting Temple and its pagoda

After recording everything I could remember, I got back up and continued down the trail. About halfway to the bottom, the trail led across a wide meadow where several horses were grazing. There was also a stone building at one end of the meadow that looked like it might be a small temple, so I walked over and knocked on the door. A few seconds later, a young man appeared. He was holding a walkie-talkie. Obviously, he wasn't a monk. He said he lived there with three other men, and they were in charge of protecting the mountain's plants and animals from poachers. He pointed at the clump of rhododendron flowers behind my ear and said it was illegal to pick the flowers. I told him I found them on the trail, which was the truth. But just to make sure, as soon as I was out of sight, I tossed the flowers into the stream that skirted the trail. A few minutes later, I caught up to the flowers where the stream formed a pool. The pool, I decided, was big enough to bathe in, which was what I did. I thus arrived back in the village of Shachih feeling as refreshed as when I left, if not more so.

It was late afternoon, and the last bus had already left, but there was a big sign at the restaurant closest to the trailhead saying FOREIGNERS WELCOME. So I sat down, and the owner's wife stopped playing mahjong long enough to produce another memorable plate of fried eggs with tomatoes and slices of wild boar. I couldn't bring myself to order the pheasant.

And so I finally ended my pilgrimage to Chickenfoot Mountain. Except for a ninety-four-year-old Tibetan lama, I hadn't seen another pilgrim on the trail—only porters. It was a rare experience in China, having a mountain to myself. And it wasn't just any mountain. With that thought, I fell asleep.

The next morning, the owner's wife woke me and said it was time to leave. The sun wasn't over the ridge yet, but I didn't argue with her. I grabbed my pack and went outside. She told me to hop onto the back of a truck that left every day as soon as it was light. Two hours later, I was back in the town of Pinchuan. And two hours after that, I was back in the big city of Hsiakuan eating er-k'uai. Pilgrims, I've learned, are protected by the gods.

大里

25. Dali

I N THE PAST, Hsiakuan was little more than a military post for con-
trolling traffic heading east to Kunming, west to Burma, north to
Tibet, or south to Thailand. Culturally and politically it was overshad-
owed by the old capital of Dali, fifteen kilometers to the north. But
times had changed, and Dali was now a provincial backwater, while
Hsiakuan had become home to nearly half a million people, making it
the biggest urban center in the western half of Yunnan. The city's new
status was evident at the new museum at the edge of Erhai Lake, and
I decided to visit it after returning from Chickenfoot Mountain while
still munching on an er-k'uai. The museum was huge. In fact, it was
so huge, it was hard to imagine how they were going to fill it. Half the
halls were empty, and those that weren't relied heavily on photographs
and maps as the heart of their displays. Except for a modest collection
of bronze drums and Buddhist religious paraphernalia unearthed from
pagodas in the area, the only other items of note were several house
interiors that recreated the living conditions of the local ethnic groups.
But there weren't any signs indicating which group they belonged to. I
finally gave up and caught a pedicab back to my hotel, where I went to
bed early. I was all tuckered out from the mountain. And in the spirit
of my tuckeredness, the next morning I decided to conserve my strength
and joined a busload of tourists on the one-day tour of Yunnan's ancient
capital to the north.

Dali was also the ancient home of the Pai. In 1990, there were more than 1.5 million Pai living in China, and 80 percent of them were living within two hundred kilometers of Dali. As for how long they had been living there, and where they came from, the Pai tell it like this: a long time ago the earth was covered by a great sea whose waves rolled and crashed and sent spray up into the sky. And one day the waves rolled and crashed a little harder than usual, and the spray went a little higher than usual, and it tore a hole in the sky. Two suns slipped through the hole and began whirling around the heavens crashing into each other, and their sparks created the stars. Then the smaller of the suns cracked. Its shell became the moon, its core fell into the sea, and the sea began to boil—and the dragon who lived in the sea got mad and swallowed the sun. But the sun was too hot, so the dragon spit it out, and the sun went hurtling through the air and crashed into the mountain that held up the sky and broke into a million pieces. The pieces that continued to sail through the air became clouds, the pieces that remained suspended became birds, the pieces that fell on mountains became plants, the pieces that fell into valleys became animals, the pieces that fell back into the sea became fishes, and the core that remained fell into a cave and split in two. The left half became Lao-t'ai, the first woman, and the right half became Lao-ku, the first man. And they gave birth to ten sons and ten daughters, and their descendants became the ancestors of the Pai.

As far as the recorded side of the story goes, the ten tribes that traced their descent from the ten sons and ten daughters of Lao-t'ai and Lao-ku united in 737 AD under the southernmost tribe, and they built their first capital at a place called Taiho near the south end of Erhai Lake, not far from Hsiakuan. But this first capital was soon abandoned, and a second capital was built at Dali a few kilometers to the north. It was also about this time that the descendants of Lao-t'ai and Lao-ku began calling themselves Pai and their kingdom Nanchao. It was also about this time that the Chinese emperor bestowed on the Pai king the title: King of the Land South of the Clouds, or Yunnan.

As time went on, the kingdom of Nanchao began to expand its borders until it reached as far as Vietnam and Thailand to the south,

Burma to the west, Kuanghsi to the east, and Szechuan to the north. The kingdom lasted two hundred years, until 937, when one of its generals rebelled and established a new dynasty, also with his capital in Dali. And this second dynasty lasted 350 years, until Kublai Khan invaded the Southwest in 1253. While the Great Khan led the attack from the north, he sent part of his forces to the west, and they surprised the Pai army by floating down the Chinsha River—the uppermost reaches of the Yangtze—on goatskin rafts and outflanking them. Ever since then, Dali and the rest of Yunnan have been part of China.

A few minutes after leaving Hsiakuan, the one-day tour passed its first relic of Dali's ancient past. Three hundred meters from the side of the road stood a lone pagoda. Most pagodas contained the remains of ancient worthies, but this one was built to commemorate a snake and, of course, had a story to go with it.

A long time ago, the Dali area was terrorized by a python as big as a whale. This cousin of the Loch Ness monster swam around Erhai Lake, swallowing whole fishing boats and snacking on herds of cattle and villagers along the shore too slow to get out of its way. Even the king's soldiers were unable to kill it, and no one knew what to do. Finally, a young stonecutter by the name of Tuan Ch'ih-ch'eng came forward with a plan, and the king agreed to provide him with whatever he needed.

First, Tuan had the king's blacksmiths make him a special suit of armor and had it fitted with hundreds of long, razor-sharp knives. When he put it on, it made him look like a human porcupine. Then he marched down to the lakeshore where the python was dozing, and he stabbed the python with a sword. The python was so huge, the sword had almost no effect, other than to rouse the creature from its slumber. It was angry at being disturbed and opened its mouth, and in one gulp it swallowed Tuan Ch'ih-ch'eng. It was a big mistake. The knives attached to Tuan's suit of armor cut through the lining of the python's throat and stomach, and in less than an hour the python bled to death. Unfortunately, Tuan Ch'ih-ch'eng also died before the townspeople could cut open the python's stomach, and he was buried in the nearby foothills. Meanwhile, the python was cremated, and its ashes were mixed with mud to

Dali's South Gate

make bricks, which were used to build the lone pagoda we passed just outside Hsiakuan on our way to the ancient town of Dali.

A few minutes after passing Snake Pagoda, we passed another structure in the foothills. According to our guide, the building contained a stone stele erected there 1,200 years ago to mark the location of the first capital of the kingdom of Nanchao. Since this was the one-day tour, and not the two-day tour, we passed it by and a few minutes later parked outside the South Gate of Dali, the kingdom's second capital.

Our guide told us we had thirty minutes to see the city's ancient gate and its main street. As soon as we stepped outside the bus, we were overwhelmed by a dozen Pai women trying to sell us all sorts of trinkets and pseudo-antiques. They chased us as far as the town museum, all the way through the gate and past a gauntlet of shops selling Dali's famous tie-dyed clothes. But by the time we got to the museum, our thirty minutes were up, and it was time to return to the bus.

Our next stop was more memorable. In fact, it was the most memorable stop in the Dali area: three white pagodas north of the old city wall,

Dali's three pagodas

towering beneath the jagged, snowy peaks of the Tsangshan Mountains. The central, seventy-meter pagoda was built in the eighth century, shortly after Dali became Nanchao's second capital. And the two smaller, forty-meter pagodas were built on either side a century later. The temple they were once part of was long gone, but the pagodas were still there, their white towers shimmering against the backdrop of dark mountains and sunlit clouds that stretched the entire length of Erhai Lake. This time we didn't even get thirty minutes. C'est la tour. We continued north, and twenty kilometers later stopped again at Butterfly Spring.

This time our guide gave us a whole hour. We followed her along a well-worn path, past a dozen stalls selling tie-dyed clothing, to a spring at the foot of the Tsangshan Mountains. The spring was in the middle of a park, and its crystal water was full of the small coins the Chinese throw at everything for good luck. Above the spring, a huge tree branch stretched across the water, supported at several places by cement pillars. On closer inspection, the tree branch also turned out to be made of cement and covered with tar. And on the tar someone had stuck pieces of tree bark and the occasional piece of moss. It was obviously meant to replace a branch that had broken off, but it was a strange way to try to maintain appearances.

A young couple asked me to take their picture in front of the spring while they added two more coins to the thousands of silver disks already at the bottom of the spring. After I took their picture, we listened as our guide told us about two lovers who came there a long time ago. Their parents, she said, refused to let them marry, and they jumped into the spring and reemerged as a pair of yellow butterflies. Millions of their descendants were said to cover the trees and bushes every spring. At least they did, until the local farmers started using pesticides that killed all the caterpillars. The local government, according to our guide, had since banned the use of these death weapons in hopes of encouraging the butterflies to return. But the only butterflies we saw that day were on the tie-dyed clothing for sale.

After our hour at Butterfly Spring, it was time to visit Erhai Lake. Erhai is the second-largest lake in Yunnan, second only to Kunming's Tienchih Lake. But Erhai is much deeper, with an average depth of fifteen meters, compared to Tienchih's five. Its history is also deeper. When the kingdom of Nanchao ruled this area 1,200 years ago and first established the dominance of the Pai people, the official in charge of compiling the kingdom's history wrote that the ancestors of the Pai lived in the mountains and were led through an otherwise impenetrable forest by a pair of cranes that showed them a secret path leading to Erhai Lake. The Pai have been there ever since. Nobody knows who lived there before the Pai, but whoever they were, they left behind the story that the lake was originally, in fact, the eldest daughter of the King of Jade Dragon Snowy Mountain. I had already met the king's youngest daughter on Chickenfoot Mountain. She became a waterfall. The eldest daughter, it turns out, became a lake.

Archaeologists, of course, have a different story. Now that they have begun to study this part of China, it has become increasingly clear that the Neolithic people who inhabited this region were related to others who lived in eastern Tibet. In fact, Dali straddled the main trade route connecting Tibet with Southeast Asia. On the way to the lake, our tour stopped in the town of Hsichou, on the lake's western shore, where we could still see the old mansions owned by the merchants who controlled the Dali part of that trade during the nineteenth and twentieth centuries. The Tibetans wanted spices and tea, and the Chinese wanted animal skins and animal organs with medicinal uses.

After walking around Hsichou for thirty minutes, we finally proceeded to the lake itself, where we waited for the boat coming from the southern end to arrive and disgorge its load of tourists. While we were waiting, I walked down to the shoreline and inspected a very strange-looking craft still under construction. It was a double-masted boat shaped like a gourd, with sides that narrowed at the middle. The men building it said it was for hauling blocks of marble quarried along the lake's precipitous eastern shore. Apparently, the narrow part expands when the boat is

Boat for carrying marble under construction

loaded, preventing the sides from cracking under all the weight. It was an ingenious solution.

When our own boat finally arrived, it turned out to be far less interesting. It was your basic barge with a two-storey cabin. We climbed aboard and began our cruise with a lunch of vegetables and rice. Immediately after lunch, my fellow passengers broke out cards and played poker and bridge for the rest of the trip, interrupting their games just long enough to take the occasional picture of each other standing in front of some scenic spot.

One such spot was the small rocky outcrop known as Little Putuo Island. Big Putuo Island is a much larger island off the coast of China in the East China Sea not far from Shanghai. It's the sacred home of Kuan-yin, the Bodhisattva of Compassion. Erhai Lake's Little Putuo Island is about as big as a basketball court, and it's also the home of Kuan-yin—apparently her winter home. Occupying most of the island is a shrine hall devoted to her. The view of it floating in the lake was lovely. In fact, the island and its shrine were the most photographed

Little Potuo Island

scene in this part of China, next to Dali's three pagodas. I don't know if Kuan-yin ever visited, but it definitely looked like the vacation home of somebody connected with the gods.

After a picture-taking stop at Little Putuo, we continued down the east coast of the lake to another shrine: Lochuan Temple, one of the oldest temples in the Dali area, where we also stopped just long enough for visitors to scramble ashore and take pictures. I was glad that I didn't make joining tours a regular part of my trip. Our tour thankfully ended an hour later at the southern end of the lake. I took a pedicab back to my hotel and wasted no time in moving my operations from Hsiakuan to Dali.

Dali was one of the best places in all of China for the ancient pastime of doing nothing. There really weren't that many such places in China where travelers could relax in a traditional town and enjoy the companionship of fellow travelers and share information about the trail. The only other such places I knew of were the cafés of Yangshuo south of Kueilin and the Tai hostels and restaurants of Chinghung, both of which I had already visited.

On this occasion, I dropped my bags at Dali's old Number-Two Guesthouse, had a shower, walked across the street to the Tibetan Café, and ordered a Katmandu steak and a double shot of Johnny Walker. Yes, indeed, Dali was definitely an oasis. The steak was huge, the scotch was from Scotland, and for dessert I had a pancake covered with melted chocolate, washed down with a cup of cappuccino. The café's owner, I learned later, had paid his dues in Katmandu and was clearly familiar with the needs, or at least the appetites, of foreign travelers.

While I'm on the subject of food, I would like to pass on a recipe I extracted from the chef at the Nanchao Hotel in Hsiakuan the previous day. The hotel's restaurant was down an alley in back of the hotel, and half the tables had been reserved for a wedding party. The bride and groom, in fact, were standing at the door waiting for guests. Since it would have seemed impolite to ignore them, I offered my congratulations but turned down the chewing gum and cigarettes.

I don't know if I've mentioned it before, but one way for a stranger to choose a good restaurant in China is to find out where the locals hold their wedding banquets. To the Chinese, nothing is more important than food, and the better the food they can offer their guests, the greater their self-esteem. So I entered the Nanchao Hotel's restaurant assured I was about to enjoy a good meal. I was not disappointed. It was great. Afterwards, I asked my waitress if I could talk to the chef. A few minutes later he came out, and I told him how much I enjoyed the dishes, especially the soup. Before he returned to his kitchen, he told me the secret to his soup.

First, you boil some water. Of course, tap water in some areas is guaranteed to ruin a soup, so you might want to splurge on bottled water—just to make sure. Anyway, into this pot of boiling water, pour a couple of well-beaten eggs. Let the eggs cook for a few seconds, and I mean seconds, not minutes, then throw in a bunch of chopped tomatoes, stir a couple of times, and that is it. Yes, that is it. No salt, no soy sauce, nothing but eggs without their shells, tomatoes without their stems, and good water. But one word of warning: don't let the tomatoes cook. Freshness is the key to this soup. Also, you might want to experiment with different kinds of tomatoes. Other than that, the Nanchao Hotel's egg-and-tomato soup is pretty much a foolproof recipe and deserves a place in any South of the Clouds cookbook.

Meanwhile, back at the Tibetan Café, the next morning I continued my indulgence and ordered the Dalai Lama Breakfast, which consisted of a big bowl of rolled oats, fruit and yogurt, and an old copy of the London *Sun* with the headline: "Alien Wins Seat in Parliament." That and a couple more cups of cappuccino and some helpful advice from the waitress got me rolling. I went outside, rented a bicycle, and pedaled down the town's main street. I wanted to visit a few sights in the Dali area that I had missed on the one-day tour. The first sight was actually a hundred sights, which was how many shops there were lining the town's main street that specialized in tie-dyed clothing. This time I stopped long enough at one of them to order two blue-and-white-striped robes for friends in Hong Kong and a shirt for myself. I've been wearing that shirt on special occasions for over twenty years. I wear it whenever I do a poetry reading or give a talk. It's covered with little tie-dyed butterflies and never fails to remind me of Dali.

Afterwards, I continued down the main street to the town museum, the door of which I had reached but hadn't had time to enter during the previous day's tour. I soon realized why the tour hadn't included it. The museum in Hsiakuan had laid claim to most of the relics from the Dali area in order to fill its cavernous halls, and the Dali Museum had to make do with what the other museum left behind. Still, it left behind two of the most beautiful pieces I had ever seen. On the second floor of the main hall were two one-meter-high Sung dynasty statues, each carved from a single block of wood. They were meant to represent Samantabhadra, the Bodhisattva of Skillful Means, astride an elephant, and Manjusri, the Bodhisattva of Wisdom, seated on a lion. A few flecks of gold and red were the only evidence that they had once been painted. But the real art was the carving. They looked as stately and serene as the trees from which they were carved eight hundred years ago.

In another hall, I found something more recent, a collection of silk-screen paintings by local artists. I was captivated by one of a Pai woman holding some fruit. The painting was done mostly in red, and it was called, appropriately, *Red Fruit*. The price was 200 dollars, which was an awful lot of dollars. I couldn't talk myself into buying it. But it was beautiful, and I wish I had overcome my tightwad nature. All I could think of as I pedaled away was the girl with the red fruit—the wooden serenity of the museum's two bodhisattvas had already become a distant memory.

As I proceeded out of town through the South Gate, I then turned right and pedaled up a long, sloping road to a solitary pagoda. The temple that once surrounded the pagoda had been destroyed and was in the process of being rebuilt. Somewhere between the pagoda and the snow-capped peaks of the Tsangshan Mountains behind it was the Kublai Khan Memorial Stele that recorded the Mongol leader's exploits in the Yunnan area. I asked the workmen if they knew where it was. They just shrugged, and I returned to the main road and continued pedaling south.

After about four kilometers, I stopped again, this time at Kuanyin Temple, which also served as the headquarters of the local Buddhist association. It wasn't a very big temple, but its shrine halls featured some fine stone work, including a pavilion made entirely of marble. Over the centuries, Dali has become so famous for the marble quarried in the surrounding mountains that its name has come to mean "marble."

Residential door in Dali

Small temple outside Dali

Just past Kuanyin Temple, I turned off one last time and pushed my bicycle a kilometer or so up a cobblestone road to another small temple set in a grove of cedars. It was a lovely place, and I sat down outside and tried to enjoy the fruits of my climb, namely the view of the lake below and the mountains behind. But all I could think about was a chocolate-covered pancake at the Tibetan Café, and getting there was all downhill.

Like Yangshuo, Dali was home to half a dozen cafés catering to foreign travelers, and the Tibetan Café was the most popular when I was there. Maybe it was the orange-crate decor, or maybe it was the Miles Davis tapes, or maybe it was the chocolate pancakes and the steaks, or maybe it was Joe, the American from Wisconsin who helped run the place when the owner wasn't there. Whatever it was, it attracted most of the foreigners who passed through town long enough to sit down. And they usually stopped by at least once a day until they left. Among the café's regular customers, I met a Japanese student who had come all the way from Tokyo for Dali's Third Month Fair, which was still two weeks away. Rooms, he said, were impossible to find then, and he wanted to make sure he had a place to stay.

Dali's Third Month Fair is the biggest event of the year in this part of China, and it attracts several hundred thousand people. It begins every year on the fifteenth day of the third lunar month, which is usually in early April, and lasts a week. It has been held on the slopes of the Tsang-shan Mountains just outside of town for more than a thousand years, ever since one of the Dragon King's daughters looked up at the sky one moonlit night a long time ago.

Her name was Lung-san. She was the third daughter of the dragon who lived in Erhai Lake, and she was married to a fisherman. One night when the moon was full, she looked up and wondered what was happening on the moon. She called one of her father's dragon attendants out of the lake and asked him to carry her and her husband to the moon to investigate. When they got there, they discovered a huge fair in progress. Thousands of moon people were gathered around a big tree, and they were singing and dancing and telling stories and holding contests of skill and strength and selling products that grew on the moon or things moon people made. The husband and wife had never seen anything like it, and after they returned to their own village where Dali now stands, they decided to hold the same kind of fair around a big tree that grew at the foot of the nearby mountain. And the Third Month Fair has been held there ever since at the edge of town. The fair is to the Pai of Dali what the Water-Splashing Festival is to the Tai of Hsishuangbanna, and it is no coincidence that both are held at the same time. Like the Tai, the Pai are Buddhists, and the fifteenth day of the third lunar month is the birthday of Kuan-yin, the Bodhisattva of Compassion. The fair begins with a big Buddhist ceremony at the temple in front of the town's three white pagodas. Unfortunately, Dali's Third Month Fair was still two weeks away, and, as usual, I had a date with a bus.

石寶山

26. Shihpaoshan

I ROLLED OUT OF bed the next morning and walked from the old Number-Two Guesthouse to the fancier Number-One Guesthouse. I had a ticket for the bus that stopped there every morning at seven o'clock on its way north. I was sad to leave my new favorite city behind, but there was still more of Yunnan to see, and I only had a few days left.

The bus was on time, and the road was good. We cruised across the Dali Plain at an incredible sixty kilometers an hour. After about thirty minutes, we whizzed past the turnoff to the village of Shaping, where people came from as far away as Cleveland and Stuttgart for the Monday market. Shaping's Monday market was the biggest weekly market in this part of China, but it was Saturday, and I didn't have two days to spare.

Two hours after passing the Shaping turnoff, we stopped in the middle of nowhere for lunch. It was only nine thirty, but the middle of nowhere included a restaurant with which the bus driver had an arrangement. And our driver wasn't alone. A few minutes later, another bus pulled up and unloaded its passengers. Since I wasn't hungry, while everyone filed inside for an early lunch, I waited outside where half a dozen vendors were selling herbal medicines, boiled eggs, fried cheese, and—what was this? There was the same man I met on my way to Chickenfoot Mountain. And he was still trying to sell the same baby owl. The only thing different was the price. It had gone from 30RMB to 100RMB. He was

Pai villagers on the way back from market

waiting, he said, for Shaping's Monday market. Obviously, the Monday market was not the cheapest place to buy an owl.

After "lunch," we all reboarded our bus and continued north. Three hours later, I got off at the town of Chienchuan, if it could be called a town. I didn't really stay there long enough to find out. A few minutes after getting off the bus, I was in the back of a tractor rolling down the highway heading back the way I had come. I was on a mission, and the tractor just happened to be going my way—for a price.

After seven kilometers, we turned off at the bus-stop village of Tiennan and headed west. My destination was the mountain of Shihpaoshan, thirty kilometers away. Since there was no public transportation or taxis in Chienchuan, I had no choice but to hire a tractor to take me there and back. The owner was a farmer, and it didn't take long for us to agree on the very reasonable price of 30RMB, or 6 dollars.

It was a memorable trip, but not one I would want to repeat, at least not the tractor part. A few minutes after leaving the highway at Tiennan, we turned off and headed southwest on a dirt road that felt like a washboard. For the next three hours, we rattled and bumped our way up and down hills and across valleys and through gorges and eventually to the top of Shihpaoshan. My bones were still rattling when I got off, and they rattled for hours afterwards. But at least I was there.

The reason I had gone to such lengths and spared no expense was that I wanted to see some of the most unique rock carvings in all of China. Like Dali, Chienchuan straddled the road between Southeast Asia and Tibet, and the people who profited from the trade had financed the carving of hundreds of Buddhist statues on Shihpaoshan. Although it was only thirty kilometers southwest of Chienchuan, visitors were few, which I found surprising.

While the farmer waited by his tractor in an otherwise empty parking lot, I proceeded down a trail to Shihchung Temple. In Chinese, "shihchung" means "stone-bell." The name came from a huge boulder next to the temple. Although the temple was still there, there weren't any monks, only a couple of caretakers. Since neither of them seemed interested in showing me around, I followed a trail that led out of the temple

Shihpaoshan and Shihchung Temple

and ended several hundred meters later just above the temple at a series of galleries built across a cliff face. The galleries were meant to protect the figures that were carved out of the rock there more than a thousand years ago. Despite the protection, time and weather had done their work, and only eight sets of carvings had managed to survive reasonably intact. Still, those that had survived were remarkable in terms of both style and subject matter.

The first two sets of carvings included likenesses of two of the kings that ruled the kingdom of Nanchao 1,200 years ago from their capital in Dali. Their stylized features and dress, as well as those of their ministers and attendants, have provided important information for those studying the period when the Pai and their allies ruled most of Southwest China. The next five sets of figures were of more interest to Buddhists, especially number six. It included a figure of a buddha seated on a lotus flower with two disciples in attendance. The sign said the figure was that of Shakyamuni Buddha, and the disciples were Ananda and Kashyapa. But the most interesting part of the scene was the deities, not the buddha and his disciples. There were eight of them, and they each had not one but several scowling, hideous faces. According to historians, this was the only place they had found such figures outside Tibet.

But the most famous set of figures and the one at which I paused longest was number eight, which had less to do with the history of the Nanchao period or Buddhism than it did with the ancient cult of procreation. It included a two-foot-high vulva on a lotus flower with two bodhisattvas in attendance. Since it was first carved into the cliff over a thousand years ago, thousands of women had lit candles and incense before that crack in the rock in hopes of producing a child from their own stony womb.

After I had lingered long enough, I continued along a side trail that led down the cliff and across a stone bridge to another cliff that faced the temple from across a ravine. There were three sets of carvings, and I had trouble locating two of them. But my persistence was rewarded. Of the two I found, the second was especially interesting. One of the carvings featured the round eyes and aquiline nose of a Persian noble. Centuries before Marco Polo passed through Yunnan on his mission for Kublai Khan, merchants and emissaries came here all the way from the Middle East via the Silk Road and across Tibet. Suddenly my three-hour ride in the back of a tractor didn't seem like such an ordeal.

The only other carvings of note on that part of the mountain were the stone likenesses of an eighth-century king and queen of the Nanchao period inside a cave. But the gate was locked, and all I could do was peer

King and Queen of Nanchao

through the bars into the gloom. Since I had seen all there was to see, I returned to the parking lot and steeled myself for another three-hour tractor ride back to Chienchuan. But before I boarded my carriage, the parking lot attendant let slip the information that the best carvings were several kilometers to the south, scattered across the mountain's northern slope. Finding them, he added, would be a problem. But problems only encourage a solution, so off I went.

From the parking lot I followed a trail that skirted the mountain's slope for about two kilometers. Then the trail disappeared, and I was on my own. The part of the slope where it disappeared was covered with boulders and Yunnan pines. The Yunnan pine is also known as the "snow pine," and it is one of the most beautiful pines in the world. Its trunk forms a spiral as it grows, and it doesn't grow very high, maybe ten meters at most. Also, its lower branches drop off as it grows, and the upper branches that remain form a dark-green canopy. I wondered why it wasn't more popular with bonsai growers. Its form was so exquisite.

Apparently there must have been a shrine on the same slope. On one of the boulders, I found the likeness of a sage, and someone had carved out a stone basin. But there was no sign of a trail. While I continued to look for anything that might suggest a way forward, I heard someone chopping wood, and I headed toward the sound. As I got closer, I could see an old lady bent over, chopping down a pine tree. The mountain was supposedly a protected area, but all around her were the stumps of snow pines. I approached to within a few meters and asked her if she could direct me to the stone carvings. She hadn't heard me approach, and she nearly fainted when she turned around. But she didn't faint. Instead, she

Yunnan snow pines

Shihpaoshan buddha statue

Shihpaoshan buddha carving

knelt down and implored me not to take her. She said she wasn't ready to die. Seeing my beard, she thought I was there to escort her to Hell.

It took several minutes, but I was finally able to convince her I wasn't there to take her to the Netherworld. She had never seen a foreigner before, much less anyone with a beard as long as mine. She said, "Well, if you're not from Hell, where are you from?" I asked her if she had heard of Los Angeles. That didn't help much either. She had never heard of Los Angeles. It took some convincing, but when it finally dawned on her that I was, in fact, not there to rip out her soul, she began to laugh, and between chuckles she told me to follow the ridge down into the ravine below. I did what she said, and thereby came upon some of the most impressive Buddhist carvings I had ever seen.

Inside the ravine there were three shrines, each with a collection of large stone buddhas and attendants, some as much as five meters high. Two of the shrines were locked, but I could see the figures inside clearly. The carvings reflected a Southeast Asian influence, especially in the draping of the robes. But the figures at the mouth of the ravine were the ones that caused me to linger the longest. They were in the open and in excellent condition. I stayed as long as I could, but the sunlight was fading, and I had to head back. When I started walking up the slope I had just come down, something else caught my eye. I looked up and found myself staring at what might have been the world's biggest vulva. It was a natural crack in the cliff about five meters high, and it was flanked by two huge stone guardians carved in relief. I struggled through the shoulder-high brush that covered the rocky slope, and when I finally reached the crack, I looked inside. If anyone had left an offering to the spirit of procreation, I couldn't see it. It was too dark. It was also getting darker outside. The sun was on its way down. I hurried back to the parking lot, where the farmer and his tractor were waiting. As I got ready to climb aboard his carryall, he said we would have to spend the night at the temple. His tractor didn't have lights.

It was hardly an inconvenience. The temple was in a beautiful setting, and the caretakers showed me and the farmer to two pine-paneled rooms overlooking Lion Pass to the north. But we weren't alone.

Shihpaoshan vulva guardian

Pai women sowing rice seeds

Another group of half a dozen travelers arrived while the caretaker was showing us to our rooms. They were from Dali, and they brought not only their own vehicle but also their own dinner—in the form of a goat. They left it with its legs tied lying in the temple's courtyard while they registered for the night. Afterwards, they slit the goat's throat, drained the blood, skinned it, and started barbecuing the carcass over an open fire. They invited me to join them, but I declined. There may not have been any monks there, but the place still looked like a temple to me. I dined instead on wild vegetables and rice.

The next morning it was clear we had spent the night on a mountain. It was so cold, the farmer had to pour hot water into his tractor's radiator before he could start his engine. The hot water worked, and off we went on another three-hour, bone-rattling ride back to the real world. The farmer who owned the tractor made his living during the slack season carrying people and materials between Chienchuan and the outlying villages. When we finally got back to town and I discovered the next bus

Pai villagers praying for a good harvest

headed north wasn't due for three hours, he invited me to join him for lunch at his home at the foot of the mountain east of town.

Chienchuan was located in a long valley between two mountains, and the foothills of both mountains were lined with small shrines and the occasional buddha statue carved out of the cliff a thousand or more years ago. My visit coincided with the annual rice planting, and after lunch I spent my remaining time in the fields where the Pai villagers were offering incense and flowers and food to the gods that watched over their rice. Even the children bowed down in respect, lest the blame for a poor harvest fall on their small shoulders. I did my part too, then boarded the last bus of the day heading north, toward Tibet.

麗江

27. Lichiang

A N HOUR NORTH of Chienchuan, the road forked. We turned east and began working our way up to a high plateau and toward the town of Lichiang. When I first planned this trip, I drew a line on my map that continued past the Lichiang turnoff to Chungtien a hundred kilometers to the north. Unfortunately, the authorities in Dali said that Chungtien was closed to foreigners. At least it was in 1992. In the past, I would have ignored that sort of restriction and tried my luck. The worst that could have happened was I might have been detained in the local jail for a day or two before being fined 100 bucks then sent back the way I had come. After three days, the authorities are required to contact a foreigner's embassy and press charges, and they usually hate to deal with the resulting paperwork. But I was running short of time and money, and the possible fine and lost time in jail made it not worth the risk.

Still, even though I wasn't allowed to visit Chungtien, I was able to read about the people who lived there. Chungtien is home both to Tibetans and Nahsi, each of whom trace their ancestry to different branches of the Chiang, who lived north and west of Chungtien as far back as 3,000 years ago. During that period, the ancestors of the Nahsi lived in the eastern part of what is now Chinghai province along the upper reaches of the Yellow River. Then, about 2,000 years ago, other branches of the Chiang and also the Han Chinese began expanding into that region, and the Nahsi began migrating south. Their Nahsi descendents have been living in northwest Yunnan ever since, or for the last 1,500 years.

In that land of high plateaus and deep gorges, the town of Chungtien held a special place in their history. Chungtien was the hometown of their greatest hero: Ting-pa Shih-lo. Ting-pa Shih-lo was born there in the eleventh century on the thirteenth day of the ninth lunar month. When he was born, all the demons gnashed their teeth in fear of what awaited them when Ting-pa Shih-lo grew up. A sorceress named K'u-sung-ma did more than gnash her teeth. She grabbed Ting-pa Shih-lo from his mother and ran off into the mountains, then she put him into a cauldron and lit a fire and cooked him for three days. When she lifted the lid, not only was Ting-pa Shih-lo unharmed—he floated up to the sky on the steam that rose from the cauldron. And he dwelt with the gods and learned the language of magic and sorcery from them.

Years later, when Ting-pa Shih-lo returned to the world, he went straight to K'u-sung-ma and said, "While I was in Heaven, I enjoyed the company of ninety-nine heavenly women. Now that I've returned to the world, I need an earthly woman, and since you're the most beautiful and most powerful woman in the world, I want you for my wife." K'u-sung-ma could hardly believe her ears, but it was an interesting proposition. She finally put aside her fears, and they were married. But it wasn't an easy marriage. K'u-sung-ma was always causing illnesses and disasters, and Ting-pa Shih-lo was always going around righting her wrongs.

Finally, it got to be too much for Ting-pa Shih-lo, and he put K'u-sung-ma in the same cauldron she had tried to cook him in when he was a baby. Only she didn't do as well. Before she expired, however, she cursed him, saying, "May you spend the rest of your days at the bottom of the sea." Not long afterwards, when he went swimming in a lake, he sank to the bottom, and nobody knew what happened to him until his disciples saw his clothing on the lakeshore. Fortunately, they guessed what had happened and attached a rock to a long cord and threw it into the lake. Ting-pa Shih-lo grabbed hold and was pulled to safety, and he spent the rest of his life helping his people. And on the eighth day of the

Nahsi women at the Lichiang market

second lunar month, Nahsi villagers come from hundreds of miles away to honor his memory at Paiti Gorge, just outside Chungtien—a town I was only able to imagine visiting.

Imaginary visits, however, can only be imagined for so long. Finally, two hours after turning off the road that led to Chungtien, the bus I was on completed its journey across a huge basin to the town of Lichiang. Like Chungtien, Lichiang is also home to the Nahsi, and it is the only place in China where foreigners can learn something about their culture. At the north edge of town there was a lovely park surrounding Black Dragon Spring. And on a hill at the edge of the park was the Tungpa Cultural Research Institute. As soon as I dropped my bag at Lichiang's Number-Two Guesthouse, that was where I headed.

Tungpa is the name of the religion begun a thousand years ago by Ting-pa Shih-lo. In the Nahsi language, the word "tungpa" means "mountain sutra." Sutras are the sacred books of Buddhism, and the religion begun by Ting-pa Shih-lo combines elements of Buddhism with the shamanism practiced by the peoples of the high plateau. But when Ting-pa Shih-lo recorded his religious insights, he created his own ideographs, which he explained to his immediate disciples and to no one else. This became known as the Tungpa script. According to the girl who guided me through the institute, there were only a handful of Nahsi left who could read and write this amazing script, with its animal heads and stick people and suns and moons. Later, I bought a copy of one of these sutras at the institute bookstore, just in case I ever needed to end a drought or stem a flood or get a berth on a Chinese train. My guide told me that in a few more years she doubted there would be anyone left to explain it to me. Transmission of the knowledge was from father to son, and none of the sons of the few remaining Tungpas were interested in learning this shamanistic approach to dealing with illness and disaster.

In addition to a traditional Nahsi house and a lovely garden, the institute included several exhibition halls featuring the ritual paraphernalia and poses as well as the art and literature of the Tungpas. One of the most interesting items was a collection of stakes covered with pictures of mythical beasts and words written in the Tungpa script. According to my guide, the stakes were driven into the ground around the house of someone who was ill or recently deceased to drive away offending spirits. Different groups of stakes were used to get rid of different spirits, similar to how acupuncture needles are used.

There was also a collection of Tungpa musical instruments. The ensemble on display was made up mostly of percussion and wind instruments, including cymbals, hand drums, even conch shells. Again, the emphasis was on chasing away demons. Oddly enough, most of the foreign ghosts who visit Lichiang make a point of dropping in at the local theater to listen to Nahsi musicians perform their traditional ghost-chasing pieces. And yet the musicians don't seem to mind that the music doesn't work. The foreign ghosts keep coming.

For the past thousand years, the Tungpas have acted as the shaman class of the Nahsi tribe, and chief among their functions has been helping the dead gain a better rebirth. Among those on whom they call to perform this feat is the mythical bird known to the Nahsi as well as to the Chinese as the P'eng. The Taoist text *Chuangtzu* begins with this line: "In the North Sea lives a fish called K'un. It's thousands of miles

Jade Dragon

long, and when it wants to go south, it changes into a bird called P'eng, which is thousands of miles wide. And the P'eng climbs into the sky until it has thirty thousand miles of wind under its wings. Only then does it head south for the Lake of Heaven." One of the institute's displays included a statue of the P'eng standing between the land of the living and the land of the reborn. And beyond the P'eng and the land of the reborn was the Mountain of Nirvana. One of the duties of the Tungpa shaman is to call on the P'eng to ferry departed spirits beyond the land of evil rebirths and lost souls to this final land of bliss.

The P'eng, it turns out, is an old friend of the Nahsi people. According to them, humankind and dragons are descended from the same father. When this father grew old, he divided the earth and sky equally among his children. But once the old man was gone, his dragon child lorded it over humankind, until the ancestors of the Nahsi called on the P'eng, which captured the dragon and banished it to the snow-covered mountains to the north.

Standing outside the institute, I couldn't miss the 5,500-meter, snow-covered peak of Jade Dragon. It had never been climbed. The wind near the summit was said to be too strong and the snow too unstable. More likely, Jade Dragon simply didn't like visitors. For those who can afford to deal with the local office of China Travel, visitors can hike to the base camps used by Japanese and American climbing expeditions that had tried and failed to find a way to the top.

The next morning, I decided to pay Jade Dragon a visit. But I opted to forego a trek to the base camps and limited my visit to Jade Peak Temple. The temple was at the foot of the mountain's southern slope and about as close as I wanted to get to the beast. There was a private bus that waited for would-be passengers every morning on Lichiang's main street in front of the town's huge statue of Chairman Mao. If enough people showed up, the driver left around nine o'clock. I was just in time to get the last seat, and thirty minutes later I was at the temple.

Several Tibetan lamas had recently been invited back to take care of the place, and I could hear them chanting in a small chapel. The chapel was closed to the public, but the lamas weren't why I was there. Five hundred years ago, someone planted a pair of camellia trees at the temple. Yunnan is the camellia's home, and the twin camellias at Jade Peak Temple are the king and queen of them all. The caretaker said he once counted more than ten thousand flowers on them, and he wasn't exaggerating. The trees were in full bloom, and there were at least that many.

A former president of the International Camellia Association had been there on three occasions to see the trees and had also been impressed. In addition to noting the incredible age and size of the two trees, he praised them as masterpieces of grafting and pruning. Indeed, the temple paled beside them. Camellias aren't the only botanical treasure of the Lichiang area. Between 1922 and 1949, the American botanist Joseph Rock set up shop in the foothills just beyond the temple. Over the course of three decades, Rock identified hundreds of new plant species and introduced them to the rest of the world. Rock was a huge man. And everything he did had to be grandiose, or else he simply wouldn't do it. He wouldn't gather plants unless he could muster an expeditionary force the size of a regiment. Everywhere he went, so did his cast-iron bathtub. His prose also tested the patience of readers. One reader with sufficient patience

Jade Peak Temple camellias

was the poet Ezra Pound. When the US government locked up Pound in a lunatic asylum, his favorite book was Rock's *The Ancient Nahsi Kingdom of Southwest China*, phrases of which litter his *Cantos*: "artemisia, arundaria, winnowed in fate's tray."

After viewing the red flowers of the temple's five-hundred-year-old camellia trees, I reboarded the van and headed back to Lichiang on one of China's most lonesome roads. Halfway there, I asked the driver to let me off. While he continued with the other passengers back to Lichiang, I followed a dirt trail to the small village of Paisha two kilometers to the west. Before Kublai Khan conquered this part of China in the thirteenth century, Paisha was the capital of the Nahsi kingdom.

Earlier, 2,500 years ago, when the Nahsi's ancestors lived far to the north in what is now Chinghai province, they supported themselves as herders. Historians say they were a branch of the same tribe from which the Tibetans are descended. Two thousand years ago, when the Huns began wreaking havoc in Central Asia, the ancestors of the Nahsi were forced to migrate south and eventually settled in the high plateau country surrounding Chungtien and Lichiang. They built their modest capital in the plain that stretched between Lichiang and Jade Dragon, and twenty minutes after setting off on foot, I arrived in what was left of it. What was left was a pair of 600-year-old temples flanking a dirt soccer pitch. Outside one of them, I met the caretaker. After offering me tea in the room that served as both his office and his bedroom, he showed me the murals the Nahsi kings had left behind.

The religion of the Nahsi is a unique blend of native shamanism, Chinese Taoism, and Tibetan Buddhism, and the six-hundred-year-old murals that still graced several of the halls were national treasures. I had forgotten to bring my flashlight or binoculars, and much of the detail was lost in the gloom. The artistry was clearly evident, but someone had taken the liberty of gouging out the eyes of most of the religious figures. Among the eyes they missed were those of over a hundred buddhas and Taoist deities that filled a series of ten panels at the back of the main hall.

In addition to the two Buddhist shrine halls, there was also a Confucian temple on the north side of the soccer pitch. I stuck my head inside briefly, but it also served as the village school, and classes were in session. In addition to the Confucian temple and Buddhist shrine halls, the only other attraction in Paisha was Doctor Ho, the area's resident purveyor of herbal cures for all that ails this mortal coil. Friends who had visited Paisha had commented on Doctor Ho's eccentric ways. Unfortunately, he was off in the hills that day gathering herbs, and I had no choice but to hitch a ride back to Lichiang on a tractor.

After showering off the temple dust, I changed into my evening wear and walked across the street to plan my next foray into the Himalayan landscape. Without doubt, the best place to plan forays was Peter's Café, next to the statue of Chairman Mao. Like similar establishments in Dali, Peter's catered to foreign travelers. However, because of its relative remoteness, Lichiang didn't get nearly as many visitors, and the cafés were limited to Peter's and a similar joint next door. While the Western-style food wasn't up to the standards of Dali's cafés, Peter's was still an oasis, and so was Crystal, the woman who ran it. She named her café after her American boyfriend, or should I say husband. At last report, Peter was back home in Homer, Alaska, chopping firewood and getting ready for winter, while Crystal was still waiting for her marriage visa to come through.

When enough foreign guests show up in town, and sooner or later they show up at Peter's, Crystal organizes a Nahsi-style banquet and entertains everyone with arias from her repertoire of Chinese and Nahsi operas. And while I was there, I was on hand for such an event. Crystal's singing was definitely better than her food. She was once the diva of the local opera company. Then, several years before my visit, she struck out on her own, and she hadn't looked back. She confided to me that she now made more money than anyone else in town. She was quite a woman. Homer, Alaska, if she ever gets there, will never be the same.

And so, in the shadow of the outstretched arm of Chairman Mao, I planned my next adventure. One adventure I considered was a trip to Shihku, which was a one-day trip by private transport or a two-day trip by public bus. Shihku was just off the main road that connected Dali with Tibet, past the turnoff to Lichiang. The word "shihku" means "stone drum," and according to local legend, the drum in question was the legacy of Chu-ko Liang's army. Chu-ko Liang served as the chief strategist of the forces that championed the dethroned emperor of the Han dynasty. And his army left the drum as a symbol of Chinese rule along the empire's western flank. Visitors can still see the drum on the Yangtze River's near shore. It was carved around 200 AD out of a huge block of marble, and 1,300 years later it was engraved to celebrate a Chinese victory over an army of two hundred thousand Tibetans with words that included these memorable lines: "heads piled up like melons, blood flowed like wine."

The place where Chu-ko Liang's army left that monument to Chinese rule was of strategic significance. The Chinese call it "the first bend of the Yangtze," because it was the first place where the river slows down and makes a 140-degree turn. That is where the Mongols crossed the Yangtze when they invaded Southwest China in the thirteenth century. It's also one of the places where the Red Army crossed the river on its Long March sixty years earlier in 1936. Just above the drum there is a memorial to the efforts of the local citizens, who worked nonstop for four days and four nights to ferry eighteen thousand members of the Red Army across. The memorial also provides a fine view of the Yangtze, where the muddy waters of the Tibetan Plateau catch their breath before plunging into the waiting darkness of Leaping Tiger Gorge.

Meanwhile, back in Lichiang, under the outstretched arm of Chairman Mao, I continued to mull my prospects. I ordered another cappuccino, relit what was left of a Burmese cigar, and read the recorded observations of previous travelers in the café's journal. One read: "Hsuan-ko is a spy. If you want to have a chop carved, avoid Hsuan-ko. He says he's a persecuted Christian, but in reality he's a policeman. He's six-feet-two and speaks good English. Don't trust that guy, especially if you have Chinese dissident friends."

Another read: "Just spent a week in Juili. Worth the trip out to be sure. Has all the flavors of Southwest China, plus a lot of Burmese and Pakistanis. Juili is also China's heroin and AIDS capital, with a fair amount of prostitution—in the hotels, not on the streets. If you do decide to do something illegal, watch out. There's lots of plainclothes police running around. Happy Trails."

Another one was signed "Stacey from New York," and it began: "I'm on my way to Dali tomorrow to be treated for rabies, and I'm scared to death. I was attacked by a vicious dog in a village near the east end of Leaping Tiger Gorge. The villagers, meanwhile, just laughed. The gorge was spectacular. Sky-high granite walls, air full of butterflies, and the raging Yangtze far below. If you take two days, like we did, you can stop at Walnut Village Inn, six hours into the gorge. From the Inn, it's another four hours to the east end, which is where I was bit. Beware. Many dogs have rabies but show no symptoms. Also, none of the hospitals in Lichiang have medicine for rabies. Was the gorge worth it? I won't know the answer till I get to Dali."

With that, I finished my cappuccino and went to arrange transportation to Leaping Tiger Gorge, which was easier said than done. There was no bus from Lichiang to the west end of the gorge, and the bus to the east end only left every four days or so. I soon discovered that the next bus wasn't due to leave for three days, and that tickets were already sold out. I returned to Peter's and ordered another cappuccino. I was becoming addicted to the stuff. This time I added a shot of Chinese brandy.

When I told Crystal about my transportation dilemma, off she went to arrange a solution. A few minutes later, she returned with a driver who offered to take me to the gorge and bring me back for 300RMB, or 60 bucks. It was a steep price to pay, but it was, after all, a 180-kilometer round-trip. To ease the burden, two other foreigners sitting in the café agreed to chip in for a one-way lift. They planned to walk through the gorge from the east end and come back to Lichiang from the other end. My goal was simply to see the gorge.

Early the next morning, we all met in front of Peter's and climbed aboard what turned out to be a government truck. It was what we called in the Forest Service a "six-pack." There was room for three in front and room for three more in back. Our driver, we learned later, had reported sick the night before, so that he could take this opportunity to make more from us in one day than he made at his job all month. Obviously, there were drawbacks with putting the means of production in the hands of the proletariat.

We left Lichiang at dawn and headed north in the direction of the snow-covered spine of Jade Dragon. Thirty minutes later, as we approached the dragon's eastern flank, the driver hit the brakes. He jumped out and took off running after a wolf. We jumped out and followed him. I don't think any of us considered what we were going to do if we caught it. Fortunately, the wolf saved us from having to come up with an answer. Even with only three legs, it easily outran us. The driver said one of its legs must have been injured in a trap, or it chewed off its leg to get out of a trap. He said there used to be lots of wolves around Lichiang. Sometimes they even came into town, but not anymore. That was the first wolf he had seen in years, which probably accounted for his mad dash. I'm not sure what accounted for ours.

In any case, we caught our breath, returned to the truck, and continued on. Just past the 23-kilometer marker, we stopped again. This time, the driver led us up a trail to the top of a forested knoll for a magnificent

Eastern flank of Jade Dragon

view of the entire eastern flank of Jade Dragon. Below its snow-covered ridge, we could see the glacier that encircled much of the mountain's 5,500-meter peak. We could have spent the day there, just gazing at the scene. But we dutifully returned to the truck.

Near the 32-kilometer marker, we passed an Yi settlement that included the office in charge of issuing permits for expeditions. But we pressed on. Finally, around the 60-kilometer marker, we began working our way down 30 kilometers of switchbacks to the Nahsi farming village of Tachu. Four hours after leaving Lichiang, we finally arrived at the gorge.

Tachu was at the bottom of a high valley that overlooked the eastern end of the gorge. While the dust settled around our truck, we entered the lonesome lobby of Leaping Tiger Gorge Hotel, which was a high-falutin name for a small but clean establishment that served as a hostel and restaurant. Rooms cost 2RMB, or 40 cents. Food wasn't as cheap, but we found the kitchen stocked with sufficient supplies to provide an excellent lunch.

Afterwards, the two foreigners who had joined me for the ride there said goodbye and headed down the trail that led to the bottom of the gorge. Meanwhile, the cook arranged for a local farmer to guide me along a trail that led three kilometers west of the village to a spot that overlooked the wildest part of the river. It was tough going, and I had to lean hard to keep from being blown back by the gale-force wind that came rushing out of the gorge. Finally, after ninety minutes, we reached the promontory that looked west toward the spot where local legend says a tiger used to jump back and forth across the river long ago. The cliffs of Jade Dragon and Hapashan are only thirty meters apart here, and it's said to be the narrowest stretch of the entire Yangtze River.

The river was forced to flow at such a high speed, the series of rapids created by the seventeen-kilometer-long defile had never been successfully negotiated in an open raft or kayak. In 1986, a Chinese team managed to get through in closed rubber barrels, but at the cost of two lives. Three years later, the surviving members of the same group tried to raft a similar stretch of the Yellow River, but their bodies were never found.

Tiger Leaping Gorge

While I was standing, or trying to stand, at the eastern end, I could see the small trail that paralleled the gorge on the north side. From my vantage point, I had a good view of the first part of the trail that the two foreigners would soon be walking. My guide said the trail was thirty kilometers long from one end to the other. He pointed to a wall of scree and boulders that loomed above the tiny path local farmers had cut into the rock. He said that was the most dangerous part of the trail. Every year people were killed by falling rock, assuming they weren't blown off into the Yangtze far below.

I was glad I was only there to look. After doing just that as long as I could, I headed back to the truck, where I found four new passengers sitting in the back seat. The driver was standing outside, and I asked him if that meant a reduction in the cost of hiring his vehicle. He said the four had been working for the past year at the local tobacco-processing unit in Tachu and were due to be transferred back to Lichiang. They were all sons of high-ranking officials in the same unit he worked for, and he had no choice. Neither did I. I climbed aboard, and we began the four-hour trip back to Lichiang. But we didn't get very far. Halfway up the road that led over the mountain, the truck's linkage snapped, and we came to a stop. The elation of visiting the gorge vanished. There were no truck parts in the village. Lichiang was ninety kilometers away, and the next bus wasn't due for two days. Another fine mess I'd gotten myself into.

The driver lit a cigarette and got out his tools, and I decided to stretch my legs. While the driver began hammering away at something, I walked down the road to inspect a new house being built by some Nahsi farmers. The foundation and walls of the first storey were made of granite blocks. And the second storey was made of hand-sawed pine planks and poles. As I approached, the men and women working on the house waved for me to join them on the second-floor rafters. They were members of the same family, and the house they were building was for one of the brothers who had recently married. It was late March, and they said this was when people built their houses: after winter was over, and before spring planting began. They said it only took a month

A Nahsi house going up

to build a house like the one I was standing on, and the materials only cost 5,000RMB, or 1,000 dollars. They said such houses usually lasted two generations.

Next to the house, they were also building a tall, windowless structure out of adobe bricks. It didn't have any windows because it wasn't meant for people, or even for animals. It was for drying tobacco leaves, one of the province's most famous products. There was a small oven at the bottom of the structure, and above that was a series of shelves for the leaves. I stuck my head inside for a closer look and heard a horn. It was the truck. The driver had fixed the linkage by hammering out a new part. The gods smiled once again on my journey, and I was back in Lichiang by nightfall.

最后一步

28. Final Leg

THE NEXT MORNING I bought a bus ticket for Chinchiang. Since the bus didn't leave until the following day, I spent my last day in Lichiang wandering through the old section of town. Lichiang wasn't much of a town until about six hundred years ago when the Mongols, and then the Chinese, wrested control of the area from the Nahsi and the mountain-dwelling Yi and turned it into an administrative center and a conduit for trade goods.

Wandering through the old section of town, I got the feeling that things hadn't changed much since the fourteenth century. Most of the women still wore traditional sheepskin jackets, with seven frog eyes on the back. I didn't ask why eyes or why seven. Maybe it was just lucky. I was tired and ready to go home. The old part of town was made up of narrow alleys and wooden houses that also served as shops. Among the local products that caught my attention were Nahsi blankets and animal pelts. But I wasn't in the market for a blanket or a hat and went back to my hotel to pack for my departure the next day.

Instead of returning to Kunming via Dali, I had decided to take the longer route via Chinchiang, three hundred kilometers to the east. Going three hundred kilometers on a bus in China isn't something to look forward to, but it was my last long-distance bus ride, and I had my earplugs, which was a good thing. My seat turned out to be right behind the driver, and the driver's horn.

The trip began auspiciously enough. The station bell rang at eight

Upper reaches of the Yangtze

o'clock, and the bus left right on time. We peeled out of the parking lot past a line of station attendants, all standing at attention. I suppose that was meant to add a bit of ceremony to the operation. But I couldn't help wondering if it wasn't a last farewell for a busload of passengers being sacrificed to the road gods. I waved back.

My seat was on the left side of the bus, and for the first part of the trip, the massive white form of Jade Dragon Snowy Mountain rode along with me, just outside my window. There wasn't a cloud in the sky, and the mountain looked somewhat embarrassed to be so completely exposed. Jade Dragon is the easternmost peak of the Himalayas, whose westernmost peaks extend all the way to Pakistan. Considering the height of the peaks to the west, many of which exceed 7,000 meters, Jade Dragon is relatively short at 5,500. But try to tell that to mountain climbers.

The mountain soon disappeared, and the road suddenly plunged into a huge gorge carved out by the Yangtze as it wound through a deforested landscape. We switchbacked our way down to the bottom, crossed the river, then switchbacked our way back up the other side. The government liked to make a big deal about its efforts at reforestation. But other than a few scraggly willows, I didn't see a single tree.

The source of the Yangtze was a thousand kilometers to the west in Chinghai province, but I was still traveling along its upper reaches. Nowadays, this section is known as the Chinsha, or Golden Sand, River. The name refers not to the river's color, but to the gold eroded out of the adjacent canyons and carried into its waters by spring rains. Along the river's shores, I could see groups of black-skinned men sifting through the mud looking for nuggets and flecks of gold.

While the river dreamed of the East China Sea, I nodded off and dreamed my own dreams. Whatever they were, they were shattered when we stopped in the town of Panchihhua. "Panchihhua" means "vine flower." Apparently the name was meant to describe the town's construction along the cliffs above the Yangtze. The vine part was apt, but the flower part was a misnomer. Panchihhua was the ugliest town I had seen anywhere in Southwest China. It looked like something an animal had dug up and gnawed on. Vine flower, indeed. Fortunately, we only stopped long enough for a pee break and to take on a few more passengers. An hour later, we arrived in Chinchiang. Chinchiang's reason for existence was its train station, which linked it with Chengtu to the north and Kunming to the south. Inside, I managed to buy a ticket on the local heading south the next morning, and then retired across the street to one of the worst excuses for a hotel I had ever seen, much less spent the night in. I was nearing the end of my trip and beginning to whine. At least I had a room, and at least the room included a bed. The hallways were lined with less fortunate travelers sleeping on cardboard. And at least I got a seat on the train the next morning. One of the railway station employees mercifully let me board early, otherwise I would have had to fight for a place to sit on the floor. Not only did I get a seat, the conductor shooed people from the seats across from me, so that I could stretch out my legs. It was an odd privilege, and I felt embarrassed depriving other passengers of a place to sit. Still, I tried my best to enjoy

Riding the train along the Chinsha River

the unusual opportunity of having more room than I needed—a rare treat, indeed, on a train in China.

It was a leisurely ride, too. For the first two hours, we skirted the muddy, dawn-streaked waters of the Golden Sand, and must have passed through a hundred tunnels as we followed the river south into open country and back into Yunnan (Panchihhua and Chinchiang were in Szechuan). We were following the same path taken by Marco Polo when he visited Yunnan at the Great Khan's request in 1287. There I was, seven hundred years later, arriving with my Italian predecessor at a place called Huangkuayuan, or Cucumber Garden.

Outside the station, I jumped in a van and headed for the province's second-most-famous natural wonder: its Earth Forest. Yunnan's Stone Forest was more famous, primarily because of its proximity to Kunming, but the Earth Forest was equally amazing, though geologically different. It covered an area of fifty square kilometers in the western half of a region known as the Yuanmou Basin. Yuanmou was the name of the largest town in the area, but it was thirty kilometers away.

Like the Stone Forest, the Earth Forest was also the result of water erosion. But in this case, the eroded forms were those of much softer sedimentary rock, and in some cases they amounted to little more than dirt pinnacles. The forest entrance was six kilometers from the main highway on a road that was almost as eroded as the forest itself. Thankfully, it was only six kilometers and not thirty, like the road leading to Shihpaoshan that I had had to travel by tractor. A sign at the entrance explained that the landscape was formed during the Pleistocene a million years ago, and its formation wasn't entirely unrelated to man's presence in the area.

After the van dropped me off, I walked through a gate that announced I was entering a protected area. That was nice to know. I passed up the camels and mules tethered to posts waiting for tourists like me and hiked down into the completely dry riverbed that ran through the middle of what had to be the world's driest forest. The riverbed was nothing but sand, and walking on it was difficult. My feet sank. After about an hour of slogging my way through the canyon that floods had carved, I decided I had seen enough. Even though it was early April, the sun was blazing hot, and shade was nonexistent—well, not entirely nonexistent. Just as my energy was beginning to fade, I spotted a cart and a pair of mules in the shade of a cliff. I abandoned my preference for self-reliance, and a few minutes later rode out of the Earth Forest, but not out of the Pleistocene.

The cart driver took me all the way back to Cucumber Garden, and thirty minutes later I boarded a local bus headed for Yuanmou. Yuanmou was to be my last stop, and in some ways the most important stop of all. Yuanmou was the site of man's earliest-known presence in Asia. In 1965, scientists found two human teeth at a site just south of town, and the teeth turned out to be nearly two million years old.

After disembarking at the town's lone intersection, I followed the main street several blocks until I came to a sign that announced the Yuanmou Early Man Museum. It was lunchtime, and the place was locked, but the caretaker was in the courtyard, and he led me to another

Yuanmou's Earth Forest

building reserved for visiting scholars planning to stay overnight. I wasn't exactly a scholar, but I was visiting. After a rare, but well-earned, siesta, I returned to the museum.

This time it was unlocked. Inside, I had no trouble finding the two teeth that had caused such a stir among paleoanthropologists. "Paleo" means "old," and these two teeth certainly qualified. When they were first found, they were given a date of 1.7 million years, and Yuanmou Man, as he was called, was put forward as the earliest-known human in Asia, about a million years earlier than Peking Man. Dates, though, are funny things, and not everyone was willing to accept the notion that early humans were walking around China that early. The problem was that the date was based not on the teeth themselves, but on the layer of rock in which they were found, and some scientists thought the teeth might have been carried there from somewhere else. In any case, there they were, or at least there their reproductions were, two human incisors the Tooth Fairy missed.

Unfortunately, the museum did a terrible job of presenting all the evidence or of telling the story. And there was a story worth telling. As far as early humans being out of place in China, that issue was put to rest following a number of later finds at Lufeng, a hundred kilometers south of Yuanmou. Those finds included the most numerous and complete skeletal remains found anywhere in the world, of an ape known as Ramapithecus. Most anthropologists agreed that Ramapithecus was a direct ancestor of *Homo erectus*, or early humans, and the Ramapithecus finds were given a date of 8 million years. Also, several years later, a large fossilized rock was discovered outside of Yuanmou, and it contained seven teeth belonging to *Homo erectus*. The rock was given a date of 2.5 million years, and there was no way those teeth could have gotten there after the rock was formed. That made them about the same age as the earliest *Homo erectus* finds in East Africa. Yuanmou, it turns out, was one of humanity's earliest homes. But what made Yuanmou even more special was that things in the Yuanmou area hadn't changed much since then. The mountain range east of town was still home to people whose way of life was in many ways not that different from what it was in Neolithic days.

After reviewing the evidence for man's early presence at the museum, I decided to make one last foray into the hills. Earlier, when I was walking to the museum, I passed the local marketplace and saw several members of the Yi and Miao minorities dressed in their traditional attire. I figured their villages couldn't be far away. From the museum, I followed the main street east out of town until it turned into a dirt track for mules and carts, and I began working my way across a series of dry riverbeds. Foreigners weren't supposed to visit the ethnic groups in the mountains without a permit or guide, but I didn't have time to bother with that formality. It was a Sunday, and the local government's foreign affairs office was sure to be closed anyway. I was short of time, and I wasn't about to be denied. And so I slogged my way through the gravel of the floodplain. At some point I saw a monument in the distance and went to investigate. It turned out to be the site of a Neolithic community whose members lived there five thousand years ago. It was called Tatuntzu. According to the explanation on the stele erected at the site, among the items uncovered in its graves were sea-tortoise shells that were used for divination. The shells proved the existence of a trade route to the South China Sea a thousand kilometers away as well as the similarity in religious orientation among the cultures of both South and North China at the dawn of Chinese civilization. After looking at my watch, I caught my breath and headed for the mountain.

I had just enough time for one more hike. The mountain east of town called. The mountain, Liangshan, rose out of the Yuanmou Basin seven or eight kilometers away. But there weren't any roads, not even to the mountain's base. Two hours after setting out, I began climbing what looked like a trail. It was a steep climb, and I had to pause every few minutes to catch my breath and wipe off the sweat. According to my altimeter, the elevation at the base was 1,100 meters. When I finally stopped climbing, just below the summit, it read 2,500. Those 1,400 meters between the base and the summit had taken me another two hours to climb.

At one point I turned to scan the Yuanmou Basin far below and saw the glint of sunlight off something metallic. My binoculars turned up an ancient MiG jet practicing touch-and-go landings on an airstrip north of town. I could see why the authorities didn't want foreigners wandering around without a guide. As usual, I was on my own. But in this case, I was even more on my own than usual. I hadn't seen a soul for four hours, and I was beginning to wonder if I had taken the wrong trail. Then, as I crossed one last ridge, I saw a collection of mud huts. Ah, civilization, I thought, or at least something headed in that direction. But I was mistaken. A few minutes later, I entered the most deserted village I had ever been in. The only sign of life was a mean-looking dog.

The village consisted of two dozen houses built mostly of mud and thatch with windows facing inner courtyards. From outside, the place looked like a fortress. I knocked on several doors, but no one answered. Finally, I found one of the doors ajar and poked my head inside. An old lady was standing in a cloud of flies using a pitchfork to make fertilizer by mixing manure with straw. I waved, but she seemed to be blind. Her eyes were covered with cataracts. A yodel was more successful, and I asked her if I could get a drink of water. She nodded and shuffled off

Lisu women coming back from market

then came back with a dipperful of the sorriest-looking drinking water I had ever seen. The surface was covered with a white scum. But I was so thirsty, I asked for seconds. The name of her village, she said, was Kachin. And it was home to nearly a hundred Lisu. The last time anyone counted, there were half a million Lisu in China, and nearly all of them were living in the mountains of northwest Yunnan. But this was my first encounter. Apparently, they preferred the higher slopes.

I asked where everyone was and finally solved the mystery. It was market day, and everyone had gone down the mountain to Yuanmou. The old lady couldn't see or walk, so she got left behind. I toyed with the idea of asking to spend the night. I didn't know anything about the Lisu and wanted to learn more. But the flies were simply too much, and the thought of returning to civilization finally won out. I headed back to town, and for the next three hours I thought about nothing except what I would have for dinner and how good a cold beer would taste. Along the way, I met some of the Lisu coming back, some of them on mules. I just nodded. I didn't have time for anything more.

I made it back to Yuanmou just as the last rays of sun were streaming down the main street and washed away the trail dust with every cold beer I could find, all three of them. The next morning, I boarded a train bound for Kunming. It had been quite a trip. My bag was heavier, and I was lighter. I figure I lost ten pounds, thanks to my one-beer-every-other-day diet. I didn't feel like the same person who boarded that hydrofoil in Hong Kong and churned up China's West River to Wuchou.

When I first started recording my recollections of this trip, I thought about entitling them: *In the Land of Myth*. Chinese history began nearly five thousand years ago with the Yellow Emperor, but it didn't make it this far south until less than a thousand years ago, when from his Pleasure Dome in Xanadu, Kublai Khan dispatched his friend Marco Polo to see what the Southwest was like. There have been many travelers since then, including China's most famous travel diarist, Hsu Hsia-k'o. This was Hsu's last trip. But I hoped it wasn't mine. Hsu contracted lacquer poisoning and died shortly after returning home. Thanks to advances in transportation and the general deforestation of the region, I was more

fortunate. As my train chugged into the final range of mountains sep-
arating me from Kunming, it passed one last monument on a hillside
outside the town of Lufeng. Backlit in the morning sun was a statue of
Ramapithecus, our ape ancestor, who preceded me there by eight million years. I hoisted an early-morning beer I had bought in Yuanmou
for the train ride and congratulated myself on making it back alive. I'll
have to do this again, or so I thought at the time.

Lexicon

THE FOLLOWING LIST includes the modified Wade-Giles romanization used throughout this book for Chinese names, places, and
terms. In each entry, the Wade-Giles romanization is followed by the
Pinyin romanization and the traditional Chinese characters. Although
the Wade-Giles system is no longer fashionable, it was designed as a
compromise for speakers of various European languages in the mid-
and late nineteenth century, while the Pinyin system was designed for
Russian speakers in the mid-twentieth century.

WADE-GILES	PINYIN	CHINESE
A-hei	Ahei	阿黑
A-ka La-yu	Aka Layu	阿卡拉玉
a-lo-han	a-luo-han	阿羅漢
A-lu Chu-tzu	Alu Juzi	阿呂舉茲
A-p'i K'ao-k'ao	A-pi Kao-kao	阿披考考
A-shih-ma	Ashima	阿詩瑪
Ailing	Ailing	矮嶺
Aini (tribe)	Aini	愛伲
Aka (tribe)	Aka	阿卡

WADE-GILES	PINYIN	CHINESE
Anning	Anning	安寧
Anshun	Anshun	安順
ao-ma la-na	aomalana	奧瑪拉那
Chang Ch'i-yun	Zhang Qiyun	張其昀
Chang Hsueh-liang	Zhang Xueliang	張學良
Chao-han	Zhaohan	召罕
Cheng Ho	Zheng He	鄭和
Chengtu	Chengdu	成都
Chengtzu	Chengzi	城子
Chengyang	Chengyang	程陽
Chenyuan	Zhenyuan	鎮遠
chi-ba-t'ou	ji-ba-tou	吉巴頭
Ch'i-chieh	Qijie	七節
Chiahsiulou	Jiaxiulou	甲秀樓
Chiang (tribe)	Jiang	姜
Chiang Kai-shek	Jiang Jieshi	蔣介石
Chiang-liang	Jiangliang	姜良
Chiang-mei	Jiangmei	姜美
Chiang-yang	Jiangyang	姜央
Chianghsi	Jiangxi	江西
Chiangti	Jiangdi	江底
Chienchuan	Jianchuan	劍川
Chih-ko A-lung	Zhige Along	支格阿龍
Chih-kuang	Zhiguang	智光
Ch'ih You	Chiyou	蚩尤

WADE-GILES	PINYIN	CHINESE
Ch'ih-sung	Chisong	赤松
Chihchin	Zhijin	織金
Chilintung	Qilindong	麒麟洞
Chin-feng Lo-k'a	Jinfeng Luoka	金風洛卡
Chinchiang	Jinjiang	金江
Ch'ing (dynasty)	Qing	清
Chingchen	Jingzhen	景真
Chinghai	Qinghai	清海
Chinghung	Jinghong	景洪
Chinglungtung (cave)	Qinglongdong	青龍洞
Chinlingshan	Qinlingshan	黔靈山
Chinsha	Jinsha	金沙
Chinting	Jinding	金頂
Chinuo (tribe)	Jinuo	基諾
Chitzushan	Jizushan	鷄足山
Chiungchussu	Chiongzhusi	筇竹寺
Chiuyi	Jiuyi	九嶷山
Chou (dynasty)	Zhou	周
Chu Te	Zhu De	朱德
Chu-ch'eng	Jucheng	居城
Chu-ko Liang	Zhuge Liang	諸葛亮
Chuang (tribe)	Zhuang	壯
Chuangtzu	Zhuangzi	莊子
Chuhsiung	Chuxiong	楚雄
Chungching	Chongqing	重慶

WADE-GILES	PINYIN	CHINESE
Chungtien	Zhongdian	中甸
Chuo-miu	Zhuo-miu	卓繆
Chusheng	Zhusheng	祝聖
Dali	Dali	大理
E-jung	Erong	額蠑
er-k'uai	erkuai	餌块
Erhai	Erhai	洱海
Fangkuang	Fangguang	放光
Feiyuntung	Feiyundong	飛雲洞
Fuchien	Fujian	福建
Ha	Ha	哈
Hainan	Hainan	海南
Han (dynasty/ethnic group)	Han	漢
Hani (tribe)	Hani	哈尼
Hapashan	Habashan	哈巴山
Heng	Heng	哼
Hengyang	Hengyang	衡陽
Ho (surname)	He	和
Hokou	Hekou	河口
Hong Kong	Xianggang	香港
Hoping	Heping	和平
Hsiakuan	Xiaguan	下關
Hsiang	Xiang	湘
hsiang-ssu-tou	xiang-si-dou	想思豆

WADE-GILES	PINYIN	CHINESE
Hsiangyun	Xiangyun	祥雲
Hsichou	Xizhou	喜州
Hsilangshan	Xilangshan	西郎山
Hsishuangbanna	Xishuangbanna	西雙版納
Hsu Hsia-k'o	Xu Xiake	徐霞客
Hsu-yun	Xuyun	虛雲
Hsuan-ko	Xuange	宣哥
Hsun (river)	Xun	潯
Huaihua	Huaihua	懷化
huai-p'ai-ao	huai-pai-ao	懷派奧
Huang-ti	Huangdi	黃帝
Huangkuayuan	Huangguayuan	黃瓜園
Huangkuoshu	Huangguoshu	黃果樹
Huanglo	Huangluo	黃落
Huangping	Huangping	黃平
Huashihhsiao	Huashixiao	滑石哨
Huashoumen	Huashoumen	華首門
Huating	Huating	華亭
Huiteng	Huideng	慧燈
Hunan	Hunan	湖南
Hungfu	Hongfu	弘福
Hungshan	Hongshan	紅山
Juili	Ruili	瑞麗
Kachin	Kajin	卡金
Kaili	Kaili	凱里

Wade-Giles	Pinyin	Chinese
Kan	Gan	干
Kao (king)	Gao	高
Kowloon	Jiulong	九龍
K'u-sung-ma	Kusongma	庫松瑪
Kuangchou	Guangzhou	廣州
Kuanghsi	Guangxi	廣西
Kuangtung	Guangdong	廣東
Kuanyin	Guanyin	觀音
K'uei Hsing	Kui Xing	魁星
Kueichang (river)	Guijiang	桂江
Kueichou	Guizhou	貴州
Kueilin	Guilin	桂林
Kueiyang	Guiyang	貴陽
K'un	Kun	鯤
Kunming	Kunming	昆明
Kunyang	Kunyang	昆陽
Kuomintang	Guomindang	國民當
Lahu (tribe)	Lahu	拉祜
Langte	Langde	郎德
Lantsang (river)	Lancang	瀾滄
Lao-ku	Laogu	勞谷
Lao-t'ai	Laotai	勞苔
Leikung	Leigong	雷公
Lei-ling	Leiling	勒靈
Liangshan	Liangshan	凉山

Wade-Giles	Pinyin	Chinese
Liao (surname)	Liao	廖
Lichiang (boat/river)	Lijiang	漓江
Lichiang (town)	Lijiang	麗江
Lin Piao	Lin Biao	林彪
Linchi	Linji	林溪
Lisu (tribe)	Lisu	傈僳
Liupanshui	Liupanshui	六盤水
Liusha	Liusha	流沙
lo-han	luo-han	羅漢
lo-han-tsai	luo han cai	羅漢菜
Lochuan	Luoquan	羅荃
Losuo	Luosuo	羅梭
Lufeng	Lufeng	祿豐
Lunan	Lunan	路南
Lung-san	Longsan	龍三
Lungchiang	Longjiang	龍江
Lungkung	Longgong	龍宮
Lungmen	Longmen	龍門
Lungsheng	Longsheng	龍胜
Ma-hei	Mahei	瑪黑
Ma-niu	Maniu	瑪妞
Macao	Aomen	澳門
Man-an	Man'an	曼安
Manfeilung	Manfeilong	曼飛龍
Manlungkou	Manlongkou	曼龍扣

WADE-GILES	PINYIN	CHINESE
Manpo	Manpo	曼坡
Mao-t'ai	Maotai	茅台
meng-ni-o	meng-ni-e	蒙尼額
Mengche	Mengzhe	勐遮
Menghai	Menghai	勐海
Menghan	Menghan	勐罕
Menglun	Menglun	勐侖
Menglung	Menglong	勐龍
Miao (tribe)	Miao	苗
Ming (dynasty)	Ming	明
Mintsu (hotel)	Minzu	民族
Motung	Motong	莫通
Mu Liu-chia	Mu Liujia	姆六甲
Nahsi (tribe)	Naxi	納西
Nan-mu-han	Nanmuhan	南慕罕
Nanchang	Nanchang	南昌
Nanchao	Nanzhao	南詔
Nanking	Nanjing	南京
Nanming	Nanming	南明
Nanning	Nanning	南寧
Nannuoshan	Nannuoshan	南糯山
Nieh Er	Nie Er	聶耳
P'a-ya-t'ien	Payatian	帕雅天
Pai (tribe)	Bai	白
Pai Chu-yi	Bai Juyi	白居易

WADE-GILES	PINYIN	CHINESE
Paisha	Baisha	白沙
Paishui	Baishui	白水
Paiti	Baidi	白地
Paiyueh	Baiyue	百越
P'an-hu	Panhu	盤護
P'an-ku	Pangu	盤古
Panchihhua	Panzhihua	攀枝花
Panla	Banla	班拉
Paoching	Baojing	報京
P'eng	Peng	鵬
Pi-pen	Biben	婢奔
p'i-chiu-ya	pi-jiu-ya	啤酒鴨
Pinchuan	Binchuan	賓川
P'ing (king)	Ping	評
Pingan	Pingan	平安
Pu Lo-t'uo	Bu Luotuo	布洛陀
Pu-ling	Buling	布靈
Pulang (tribe)	Bulang	布朗
Putuo	Putuo	普陀
Puyi (tribe)	Buyi	布依
p'u-er	pu'er	普洱
Sa-sui	Sasui	薩燧
Sancha	Sancha	三岔
Sanchiang	Sanjiang	三江
Sanchingko	Sanqingge	三清閣

Wade-Giles	Pinyin	Chinese
Sani (tribe)	Sani	撒尼
Shachih	Shazhi	沙址
Shang (dynasty)	Shang	商
Shanghai	Shanghai	上海
Shansi	Shanxi	山西
Shaping	Shaping	沙坪
Shenyang	Shenyang	沈陽
Shih-lin	Shilin	石林
Shihchung	Shizhong	石鍾
Shihku	Shigu	石鼓
Shihpaoshan	Shibaoshan	石寶山
Shihping	Shibing	施秉
Shuangching	Shuangjing	雙井
Shuanghokou	Shuanghekou	雙河口
Shun (emperor)	Shun	舜
Ssu-ma Ch'ien	Sima Qian	司馬遣
Ssu-tzu Ti-ni	Sizi Dini	斯茲底尼
Ssukungtien	Sigongdian	四宮殿
Sung-en	Songen	松恩
Sung-sang	Songsang	松桑
Tachitung	Dajidong	打鶏洞
Tachu	Daju	大具
Taer	Taer	塔尔
Taheishan	Daheishan	大黑山
Tahua Miao (tribe)	Dahua Miao	大花苗

WADE-GILES	PINYIN	CHINESE
Tai (tribe)	Dai	傣
Taiho	Taihe	太和
Taihua	Taihua	太華
Taka	Daka	達卡
Talo	Taluo	打洛
Tatuntzu	Dadunzi	大墩子
Teng Hsiao-p'ing	Deng Xiaoping	鄧小平
Tien	Dian	滇
Tienchih	Tianchi	滇池
Tienchin	Tianjin	天津
Tienhsingchiao	Tianxingqiao	天星橋
Tiennan	Diannan	甸南
Tienshengchiao	Tianshengqiao	天生橋
Tientou	Diantou	甸頭
Ting-pa Shih-lo	Dingba Shiluo	丁巴什羅
Ts'ai Hsi-t'ao	Cai Xitao	蔡希陶
Tsangshan	Cangshan	蒼山
Tsaohai	Caohai	草海
Tsunyi	Zunyi	遵義
Tuan Ch'ih-ch'eng	Duan Chicheng	段赤城
Tung (tribe)	Dong	侗
Tung Lin-lang	Dong Linlang	東林郎
Tungpa	Dongba	東巴
Tungting	Dongting	洞庭
Tzu Hsi	Ci Xi	慈禧

WADE-GILES	PINYIN	CHINESE
Wa (tribe)	Wa	佤
Wangfeng	Wangfeng	王峰
Weining	Weining	威寧
Wenchangko	Wenchangge	文昌閣
Wenshui	Wenshui	溫水
Wuchou	Wuzhou	梧州
Wuhan	Wuhan	武漢
Wuyang (river)	Wuyang	無陽 – 潕陽
Yang Hu-ch'eng	Yang Hucheng	楊虎城
Yangshuo	Yangshuo	陽朔
Yao (tribe)	Yao	瑤
Yenan	Yenan	延安
Yi (tribe)	Yi	彝
Yiliang	Yiliang	宜良
Yinlien	Yinlian	銀鏈
Yuan (river)	Yuan	沅
Yuan (dynasty)	Yuan	元
Yuan Chiao	Yuan Jiao	緣覺
Yuanmou	Yuanmou	元謀
Yueh	Yue	越
Yunchushan	Yunjushan	雲居山
Yunnan	Yunnan	雲南